THE
FORTUNE-TELLER'S BIBLE

D1557618

THE
FORTUNE-TELLER'S BIBLE

THE DEFINITIVE GUIDE TO THE ARTS OF DIVINATION

Jane Struthers

STERLING

New York / London
www.sterlingpublishing.com

Library of Congress Cataloging in Publication Data Available

2   4   6   8   10   9   7   5   3   1

Published in 2007 by Sterling Publishing Co., Inc.
387 Park Avenue South, New York, NY 10016

Copyright © Octopus Publishing Group Ltd 2007
Text copyright © Jane Struthers 2007

First published in Great Britain in 2007 by Godsfield
A division of Octopus Publishing Group Ltd
2–4 Heron Quays, London E14 4JP, England

Distributed in Canada by Sterling Publishing
c/o Canadian Manda Group, 165 Dufferin Street,
Toronto, Ontario, Canada M6K 3H6

For information about custom editions, special
sales, premium and corporate purchases, please
contact Sterling Special Sales Department at
800-805-5489 or specialsales@sterlingpub.com.

Manufactured in China
All rights reserved.

Sterling ISBN-13: 978-1-4027-5225-4
ISBN-10: 1-4027-5225-3

CONTENTS

PART ONE

An introduction to fortune telling

THE ETIQUETTE OF FORTUNE TELLING

The way in which you give someone a reading is almost as important as the reading itself. This is true whether you are using tarot cards, dominoes, the I Ching, or any of the other techniques outlined in this book.

You need to create a safe, comfortable, and pleasant atmosphere in which both you and the person for whom you are giving the reading can relax. Resist the temptation to give your friend a tarot reading on a train or in the middle of a crowded café, because you will both be distracted and the reading will suffer. Ideally, you should work somewhere private, where you won't be overheard.

CHOOSE YOUR WORDS CAREFULLY

Always be very careful about what you say during and after a reading. Even if the other person claims that it's only a bit of fun and she doesn't really believe in such things, she will still be listening very carefully to what you say. Of course, she'll hope that you are going to tell her something wonderful but, above all, she'll be anxious that you are

going to reveal something that she doesn't want to hear, such as imminent bad health or a partner's infidelity. This means that you have to be very responsible in the way that you react during the reading because any negative messages from you, such as a muttered "Oh, dear!" at the runes or a wince at a cartomancy spread, will alert her that something is wrong. You might be screwing up your face because you have a cramp in your foot but unless you say so your poor friend will imagine that you've just seen something terrible.

You must be careful when putting your thoughts into words, especially if you are seriously concerned by what you see in the reading. Don't be an alarmist and don't give unsolicited advice, such as telling your

Take your time when giving a reading and try to make it a relaxing experience.

friend how you think she should extricate herself from a difficult situation. Instead, simply describe what the reading is saying but do so as constructively and responsibly as possible. Above all, don't use a reading as an opportunity to give someone a piece of your mind or to offload your feelings about particular aspects of her life. You must keep your opinions to yourself, even if you almost burst in the process.

DO READINGS ALWAYS COME TRUE?

You might imagine that a reading will always come true but in fact this isn't necessarily so. The situation described by the reading may change, perhaps because the person for whom you gave the reading alters her behavior in some way. For instance, if the reading issued a warning, she may take avoiding action that successfully improves the situation and averts the problems that the reading described. It is also possible that you may have misinterpreted the reading, so the things that you describe don't come to pass.

You should work with the person for whom you are giving the reading, so it's a two-way process.

THE EGO-LESS READING

It can be very gratifying to have someone hanging on to your every word when you give a reading. Most of us enjoy holding other people spellbound when we talk to them, and you are almost guaranteed to have an entranced audience when you give someone a reading. But don't let this go to your head!

Unfortunately, there are people whose egos get out of control when they give readings, convincing themselves that every word they utter is true. The fact is that no one, no matter how celebrated or experienced, will always make accurate predictions or interpretations. So do bear this in mind if you say something that the other person doesn't agree with or understand. Don't get drawn into an argument about it or become defensive. It may be that the full circumstances have yet to be revealed, at which point what you said will make perfect sense. On the other hand, it may simply be that you've got things slightly wrong. It happens to everyone at some point.

HOW TO GIVE GOOD READINGS

Even if you only intend to give readings to your friends and family, you want to do so in such a way that they'll enjoy the experience and, preferably, come back for more. Here are some suggestions on how you can create the right atmosphere.

SETTING THE SCENE

Before you start to give the reading you must check that you've got everything you'll need. One essential is a table, ideally at a comfortable height so you don't have to crouch over it and risk getting indigestion in the process. This table should be big enough to hold everything you'll need, especially if you are giving card readings—some of the spreads can be quite large.

Make sure that the table is well-lit so you can see what you are doing. Perhaps you could put a small lamp on the table or even light some candles, provided that you won't knock them over. Check that the chairs are comfortable and make the room as free from distractions as possible. Although some people like to give readings while playing gentle background music, this can be very distracting for the recipients of the readings, so it might be better to opt for silence. As for telephones, you should either switch them off or let your answering machine take any calls. Politely ask your "client" to switch off his mobile phone as well when he arrives.

THE READING ITSELF

When you give the actual reading, do your best to make it a two-way process. For instance, if you are reading the tarot you must say what the cards mean and do your best to link their meanings together when relevant, then ask the other person whether what you've said makes sense. Try to avoid turning the reading into a lecture in which you demonstrate your divinatory talents, especially if you are feeling nervous or under pressure to perform. Allow the other person to say what he thinks, as he may have some valuable insights to share with

Lighting candles helps to create a relaxing atmosphere, but make sure they're safe.

you that will allow you to develop your reading further. Instead of making pronouncements about the reading and being unwilling to hear what the other person thinks, encourage him to open up so the reading turns into a constructive two-way discussion.

PRESERVING CONFIDENTIALITY

Whenever you give someone a reading, you should always assure him that what is discussed between you will remain confidential. And you must keep your word! This is especially important if you are giving a reading to a friend or relative. You don't want this person to wonder if you are going to divulge all his deepest, darkest secrets to your friends the moment he has shut the front door behind him. This rule still applies weeks or even months later, even if you have the juiciest bits of gossip that you'd love to tell everyone.

You might think that this rule seems rather extreme at first, but consider this: Would you want to have a reading from someone who subsequently gossips about everything you told her, apparently in confidence? No, and neither will anyone

else once word spreads that you are an unreliable confidante.

MAKE IT FUN

Finally, make the reading enjoyable for both of you. Do your best to be as relaxed as possible because that will help put the other person at his ease. Don't be afraid to make the occasional joke, provided that it's appropriate, because laughter is a terrific way to break the ice. Encourage the other person to ask you questions and do your best to answer them responsibly.

Don't worry about drying up and forgetting what something means. If this happens, you can always say that you need to sit in silence for a couple of minutes and concentrate on the reading. Trust what comes to you and don't get in a flap about it. Your intuition will rush to your aid and, if you are lucky, it will prompt you to make some of the most perceptive comments of the entire reading. Above all, remember that practice makes perfect.

Always make it clear that whatever is said in the reading will remain between yourselves.

PART TWO

Western astrology

HOW WESTERN ASTROLOGY WORKS

Western astrology is thought to have originated with the ancient Babylonians, who observed the progress of the planets across the night sky, as well as the cycles of the Moon, and compared them with daily events.

Gradually, they noticed that there was a correlation between what happened in the sky and what took place in their lives. They began to develop this empirical knowledge and it is still practiced today. You can see its influence in your own life, even at the level of reading your daily horoscope.

SUN SIGN ASTROLOGY

What you read in the newspapers is called Sun sign astrology, and it can be a very useful way of starting to learn about astrology. It's not the whole story though, as you will discover if you have your birth chart read by an astrologer. A whole new world will then open up to you—the world of your psyche and your potential.

YOUR BIRTH CHART

When you study your birth chart, you will discover that there is a lot more to you astrologically than your Sun sign (the sign that the Sun occupied when you were born). Your birth chart is a snapshot of the positions of the eight planets in our solar system (Mercury, Venus, Mars, Jupiter, Saturn, Uranus, Neptune and Pluto, which despite its recent demotion is still considered to be a planet by most astrologers), plus the Sun and Moon, at the time of your birth.

In addition, there are the angles of the chart. The Ascendant, which describes your appearance and the way you view the world, is the degree and sign on the eastern horizon at the time of your birth. The Descendant, (opposite the Ascendant), describes the way you relate to others. The Midheaven, which is the degree and sign above your head at the time of your birth, shows what you are aiming for in life, and its opposite point, the *Imum Coeli* (or bottom of the sky), describes your roots. Together, they show exactly who you are.

This carving shows symbols from the ancient Babylonian zodiac.

ARIES
MARCH 21–APRIL 20

Ruling planet	Mars
Element	Fire
Symbol	Ram
Gemstone	Diamond
Day of the week	Tuesday
Area of the body	Head
Classic characteristics	Brave, blunt, pioneering, idealistic, enthusiastic, impatient, short-tempered, self-centered, easily bored

Aries is the first sign of the zodiac and, as a result, anyone born with the Sun in Aries has a strong competitive streak. He usually prefers to be a leader rather than a follower, and he hates to think that his progress in life lags behind everyone else's. He has a pioneering spirit that propels him into many adventures, and his endearing optimism and idealism help him to sail through life's difficulties.

These are some of the general characteristics of Aries. However, the sign is divided into three sub-sections, each of which adds a different layer to typical Arien traits.

ARIES BORN MARCH 21–30
An Arien born during these dates is doubly influenced by Mars, making him dynamic, energetic and highly motivated. He has a

burning need to make things happen, and displays a fiery temper whenever he's thwarted. This is someone who likes to be active, both in and out of the bedroom.

ARIES BORN MARCH 31–APRIL 9

This Arien is influenced by Mars and the Sun so likes to be on show, regardless of what he does in life. He needs to be appreciated and he is often drawn to a career in which he takes center stage—

sometimes literally. He also has good organizational skills.

ARIES BORN APRIL 10–20

Influenced by Mars and Jupiter, this Arien likes to look deep into life and often becomes engrossed in subjects that fascinate him and take up a tremendous amount of his time. Warm, affectionate, and expansive, he has many friends. He has a strong moral or spiritual philosophy which he likes to put into practice in his daily life.

TAURUS

APRIL 21–MAY 21

Ruling planet	Venus
Element	Earth
Symbol	Bull
Gemstone	Emerald
Day of the week	Friday
Area of the body	Neck
Classic characteristics	Loyal, determined, stubborn, affectionate, needs physical and financial security, possessive, greedy

A Taurean is the salt of the earth. She is reliable, trustworthy and loyal, with a very practical streak. It is essential for her to have financial and physical security. Very determined and sure of her own mind, she has a tendency to stand her ground and possibly even to be intransigent at times. She has a strong love of tradition, to which she can sometimes cling.

These are some of the general characteristics of Taurus. However, the sign is divided into three sub-sections, each of which adds a different layer to typical Taurean traits.

TAURUS BORN APRIL 21–30

Doubly ruled by Venus, this Taurean is kind, loving and demonstrative. She has a tremendous need for stability in her life coupled with a mistrust of change, so she'll do almost anything to preserve the status quo. Hard-working and industrious, she likes to do her best at work. She can always be counted on in a crisis.

TAURUS BORN MAY 1–10

This Taurean has a dazzling combination of Taurean practicality combined with Mercurial wit and dexterity. As a result she is much more adaptable and versatile than her fellow Taureans. She is a perfectionist and therefore works hard to get things right and goes to great pains to look good.

TAURUS BORN MAY 11–21

Immensely grounded and practical, this Taurean knows how to make her way through life. Being influenced by Venus and Saturn means she's much more ambitious than her fellow Taureans, with a strong desire to be respected and treated seriously. She can seem rather reticent and withdrawn at first, but becomes much more relaxed and very witty when she is with people with whom she feels comfortable.

GEMINI

MAY 22–JUNE 21

Ruling planet	Gemini
Element	Air
Symbol	Twins
Gemstone	Agate
Day of the week	Wednesday
Areas of the body	Lungs, arms and hands
Classic characteristics	Quick-witted, intelligent, communicative, inquisitive, lively, flexible, superficial, nervy

Light, bright and versatile, the Gemini is known as the butterfly of the zodiac. He needs continual mental stimulation because he is so easily bored. As a result, he can find it hard to concentrate for long stretches and can develop dilettante tendencies. He is endlessly curious about the world and is a born communicator.

These are some of the general characteristics of Gemini. However, the sign is divided into three sub-sections, each of which adds a different layer to typical Gemini traits.

GEMINI BORN MAY 22–31

Doubly ruled by Mercury, this person finds it hard to slow down. He loves to keep on the move, which can make it hard for him to relax. As a result he has a tendency to live on his nerves. Chatty, clever, and amusing, he has many friends and takes a great interest in other people's lives. He is so versatile that he can be successful at almost anything.

GEMINI BORN JUNE 1–10

The dual rulership of Mercury and Venus gives this person an entrancing combination of Gemini wit and Libran charm. As a result he is very popular and instinctively knows how to get on the right side of other people. He puts a lot of effort into his relationships because he values his friends and partners, who appreciate him in return.

GEMINI BORN JUNE 11–21

Ruled by the brainy combination of Mercury and Uranus, this Gemini is no slouch when it comes to using his brains. He has a strong intellectual slant, which he tends to use in every area of his life. Although he has plenty of friends, he is quite independent and self-sufficient and may prefer to live alone.

CANCER

JUNE 22–JULY 22

Ruling planet	Moon
Element	Water
Symbol	Crab
Gemstone	Pearl
Day of the week	Monday
Area of the body	Breasts
Classic characteristics	Sensitive, affectionate, needs emotional security, moody, protective, home-loving, sentimental, tenacious

Home is where a Cancerian's heart is because this person has such a strong need for emotional comfort and security. She is powerfully ruled by her feelings, which can make her very changeable. She is easily put on the defensive, sometimes seeing attacks where they don't exist. Above all, she's kind and loving, with a strong tendency to be nostalgic about the past.

These are some of the general characteristics of Cancer. However, the sign is divided into three sub-sections, each of which adds a different layer to typical Cancerian traits.

CANCER BORN JUNE 22– JULY 1

Doubly influenced by the Moon, this Cancerian has a tremendous need to feel safe and loved. She is driven by her emotions and instincts, making her very sensitive to atmospheres but also quite moody. In order to feel happy, she needs an inner circle of close friends or family whom she can trust. A happy home is essential to her well-being.

CANCER BORN JULY 2–12

The twin rulership of the Moon and Pluto gives this Cancerian strong charisma and tremendous emotional intensity. Her feelings go very deep and she has a tendency to bottle up her more difficult emotions, which can lead to nerves and stomach ailments. She has a very good memory but often holds on to grudges for years. She has a powerfully magnetic personality.

CANCER BORN JULY 13–22

Being ruled by the Moon and Neptune makes this person very sensitive, and, at times, almost other-worldly. She is much less practical than other Cancerians and is highly attuned to atmospheres, so may have strong psychic tendencies. Empathic and considerate, she delights in taking care of lame ducks but may be reluctant to let go of them again.

LEO

JULY 23–AUGUST 23

Ruling planet	Sun
Element	Fire
Symbol	Lion
Gemstone	Ruby
Day of the week	Sunday
Areas of the body	Heart and back
Classic characteristics	Proud, dignified, has good organizational skills, affectionate, creative, enthusiastic, bossy, dogmatic

Leo has an instinctive need to stand out in the crowd and he usually manages to achieve this aim through his many talents. Loving and demonstrative, he has many friends and admirers. Leo is a skilled organizer although he sometimes has a tendency to become bossy and even slightly pompous. It's essential for him to be able to express his true self.

These are some of the general characteristics of Leo. However, the sign is divided into three sub-sections, each of which adds a different layer to typical Leo traits.

LEO BORN JULY 23–AUGUST 2

This Leo is a show-stopper, thanks to the Sun's double influence on him. Talented and creative, he has plenty of reasons to be in the limelight and he doesn't like to be excluded from it. He has a tendency to be flamboyant and dramatic, and he knows that he's special. Warm, generous, and affectionate, he has legions of fans.

LEO BORN AUGUST 3–12

Ruled by the Sun and Jupiter, this Leo is broad-minded, expansive, and gregarious. He believes in making his own luck, which he often does with ease, and his vibrant personality definitely helps him. Ever optimistic and positive, he has the happy knack of recovering quickly from setbacks and trying again. Sometimes he has a tendency to be outspoken.

LEO BORN AUGUST 13–23

The combination of the Sun and Mars gives this Leo a pioneering nature and a strong fighting spirit. A born leader who needs to be in the vanguard of new projects, he can quickly lose interest in enterprises that aren't going well. Very loving, affectionate, and trusting, it can be difficult for him to learn from his emotional mistakes.

VIRGO

AUGUST 24–SEPTEMBER 23

Ruling planet	Mercury
Element	Earth
Symbol	Maiden
Gemstone	Sardonyx
Day of the week	Wednesday
Area of the body	Stomach
Classic characteristics	Modest, practical, efficient, painstaking, shy, intelligent, fussy, analytical, critical

Precise and careful in almost everything she does, Virgo is always striving for perfection. Although she can be quite critical of others who fail to meet her own high standards, she is much more critical of herself. Virgo has a very analytical streak and likes to know what's going on around her. Her innate modesty can make her seem rather cool and remote.

These are some of the general characteristics of Virgo. However, the sign is divided into three sub-sections, each of which adds a different layer to typical Virgo traits.

VIRGO BORN AUGUST 24–SEPTEMBER 2

With her double rulership by Mercury, this person is very clever with words but can sometimes hide her shyness behind her sharp wit and powerful intellect. She has a tendency to worry over small details and set herself such high standards that she can sometimes find it very difficult to settle for second best.

VIRGO BORN SEPTEMBER 3–12

This Virgo is jointly ruled by Mercury and Saturn, which gives her solidity and stability. Strongly practical and self-motivated, she is ambitious and likes to attain high status, which usually comes at a price. She has a deep need to be respected and for all her hard work to be acknowledged. Her ambitions can interfere with her private life.

VIRGO BORN SEPTEMBER 13–23

Influenced by Mercury and Venus, this Virgo is calmer and more placid than the other members of her sign. Although she is not necessarily interested in worldly success, it's essential that she shares a happy and comfortable home life with people she loves. She is warm, affectionate, and emotional, and very loyal.

LIBRA
SEPTEMBER 24–OCTOBER 23

Ruling planet	Venus
Element	Air
Symbol	Scales
Gemstone	Sapphire
Day of the week	Friday
Area of the body	Kidneys
Classic characteristics	Tactful, needs harmony, sociable, indecisive, fair, romantic, gullible, idealistic

Libra strives for balance and harmony. He's the diplomat of the zodiac and will sometimes concede arguments simply in order to restore the peace. Idealistic and romantic, he puts a lot of energy into his relationships but has a tendency to turn a blind eye to the failings of partners. It can be hard for him to reach decisions because he sees both sides to any question.

These are some of the general characteristics of Libra. However, the sign is divided into three sub-sections, each of which adds a different layer to typical Libran traits.

LIBRA BORN SEPTEMBER 24–OCTOBER 2

Blessed with a double helping of Venus, this Libran sets great store by his relationships.

He has a tremendous need for other people and becomes very lonely when he's by himself. Charming and diplomatic, he has a wonderful way with words but is quite gullible and susceptible to a pretty face or a clever turn of phrase.

LIBRA BORN OCTOBER 3–12

This Libran is ruled by a combination of Venus and Uranus, which gives him magnetic charm and charisma. Emotionally, he has a tendency to blow hot and cold, so partners are never quite sure where they stand, and he needs a certain amount of freedom even if he also craves close relationships. He has a strongly original and inventive streak.

LIBRA BORN OCTOBER 13–23

Ruled by Venus and Mercury, this Libran is a tactful and charming communicator. He's clever, chatty, and witty. He needs a partner who is lively and clever, and not just a pretty face (although that's important too). He enjoys travel, whether for business or pleasure.

SCORPIO

OCTOBER 24–NOVEMBER 22

Ruling planet	Pluto
Element	Water
Symbol	Scorpion
Gemstone	Opal
Day of the week	Tuesday
Area of the body	Bowels
Classic characteristics	Intense, strong-willed, forceful, magnetic, powerful, jealous, resentful, suspicious

Scorpio emotions go very deep, often so deep that the Scorpio herself can't begin to fathom them. This is despite the classic Scorpio tendency to analyze and probe every situation that she encounters. In fact, a Scorpio isn't interested in dealing with the superficial side of life. She has tremendous willpower, making her capable of achieving almost anything she desires.

These are some of the general characteristics of Scorpio. However, the sign is divided into three sub-sections, each of which adds a different layer to typical Scorpio traits.

SCORPIO BORN OCTOBER 24–NOVEMBER 2

This Scorpio is doubly ruled by Pluto, which makes her very powerful and driven.

Hard work holds no fears for her and she'll push toward her goals despite all the odds. She has tremendous loyalty and affection, and is very supportive of her partners. One outlet for her intense emotions is a delightfully dark sense of humor.

SCORPIO BORN NOVEMBER 3–12

Ruled by Pluto and Neptune, this Scorpio is more openly sensitive, compassionate and emotional than other members of this sign. Her feelings go very deep but she has a tendency to avoid examining any emotions that alarm or unnerve her, preferring to brush these to one side. Her powerful ambitions are tempered by a streak of altruism.

SCORPIO BORN NOVEMBER 13–22

This Scorpio is ruled by Pluto and the Moon, which gives her a tremendous emotional intensity that she tries to hide from others. A happy home life is very important to her and she needs a supportive family who can encourage her in her ambitions. She can be moody and changeable, but reluctant to say what's wrong. She's very loyal and faithful.

SAGITTARIUS
NOVEMBER 23–DECEMBER 21

Ruling planet	Jupiter
Element	Fire
Symbol	Archer
Gemstone	Turquoise
Day of the week	Thursday
Area of the body	Thighs
Classic characteristics	Optimistic, open-minded, philosophical, jovial, honest, tactless, freedom-loving, restless, intellectual

A Sagittarian is traditionally the traveler of the zodiac, whether he embarks on mental or physical journeys. Endlessly optimistic and enthusiastic, he loves rising to challenges and making plans for the future. Broad-minded and easy-going, he tends to adopt a philosophical view of life and likes to learn from experience. He is gregarious, friendly, and clever.

These are some of the general characteristics of Sagittarius. However, the sign is divided into three sub-sections, each of which adds a different layer to typical Sagittarian traits.

SAGITTARIUS BORN NOVEMBER 23–DECEMBER 2

This person is doubly influenced by Jupiter, which makes him very enthusiastic, positive, and expansive. He's blessed with a strong sense of humor that belies a need to explore life from every angle in order to understand it better. He responds well to change and can easily get bogged down if he isn't offered enough variety.

SAGITTARIUS BORN DECEMBER 3–11

Ruled by Jupiter and Mars, this Sagittarian is energetic, adventurous, and daring. He jumps at challenges, often the more difficult the better, and has a strong competitive streak. He's more hot-tempered than other members of this sign and can get quite impatient when he feels he's being held back, either by other people or by circumstances.

SAGITTARIUS BORN DECEMBER 12–21

This Sagittarian is ruled by Jupiter and the Sun, which gives him tremendous personality, confidence, exuberance and energy. It's difficult to keep him down because he's got so much to offer the world, although sometimes he can seem rather too pleased with himself. Gregarious, sunny-tempered, and humorous, he has many friends.

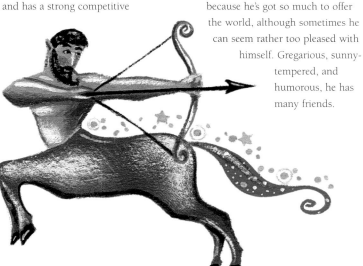

CAPRICORN
DECEMBER 22–JANUARY 20

Ruling planet	Saturn
Element	Earth
Symbol	Goat
Gemstone	Topaz
Day of the week	Saturday
Area of the body	Knees
Classic characteristics	Responsible, taciturn, hard-working, conventional, practical, ambitious, humorous, pessimistic

A Capricorn takes life a lot more seriously than other people, especially when she's young. However, she becomes more light-hearted and relaxed as she gets older, and life usually improves for her after she turns 30. She's responsible, practical, and ambitious, with a strong need to be respected for what she does. She has a delightfully dry sense of humor.

These are some of the general characteristics of Capricorn. However, the sign is divided into three sub-sections, each of which adds a different layer to typical Capricorn traits.

CAPRICORN BORN DECEMBER 22–31

With a double rulership by Saturn, this Capricorn has a very serious and conservative streak. She needs material and financial success, and to feel that she's achieved her considerable ambitions. Highly responsible and conscientious, she can become a workaholic because she's so eager to show herself in a good light. She is very loyal and trustworthy.

CAPRICORN BORN JANUARY 1–10

This Capricorn is ruled by Saturn and Venus, which give her a cool charm and a strong artistic streak. Showing her emotions is easier for her than for other members of this sign, although she'll always stop short of exuberant displays of affection regardless of how she feels inside. She loves her home and works hard at making it cozy and comfortable.

CAPRICORN BORN JANUARY 11–20

Ruled by Saturn and Mercury, this Capricorn is quick-witted, lively, and surprisingly changeable. She needs just enough variety in her life to stop her getting bored, but not enough to unsettle her. Practical and efficient, she has a perfectionist streak and a strong work ethic that helps her to get to the top of her chosen career.

AQUARIUS
JANUARY 21–FEBRUARY 18

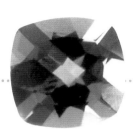

Ruling planet	Uranus
Element	Air
Symbol	Water-carrier
Gemstone	Aquamarine
Day of the week	Saturday
Area of the body	Ankles
Classic characteristics	Intellectual, independent, humanitarian, contradictory, original, honest, loyal, dispassionate

An Aquarian is the individualist of the zodiac. Each one is original, unique, and often a law unto himself, but they are all independent. An Aquarian is much better at discussing his thoughts than his emotions, and can seem quite dispassionate and cool. Nevertheless, he is faithful, loyal, and trustworthy. He is honest, sometimes to the point of bluntness.

These are some of the general characteristics of Aquarius. However, the sign is divided into three sub-sections, each of which adds a different layer to typical Aquarian traits.

AQUARIUS BORN JANUARY 21–29
This Aquarian is doubly ruled by Uranus, which makes him highly independent,

individual, and intellectual. He has a profound humanitarian streak and does his best to behave ethically. Expressing his emotions makes him feel uncomfortable, yet he is steadfast and loyal to his partner, friends, and family. He loathes sentimentality and insincerity.

AQUARIUS BORN JANUARY 30–FEBRUARY 8

Ruled by Uranus and Mercury, this Aquarian is chatty, lively, articulate, and inquisitive. He's very interested in what makes other people tick and is an excellent communicator. He's much more flexible and adaptable than other members of this sign, and needs plenty of mental stimulation and changes of scene to keep boredom at bay.

AQUARIUS BORN FEBRUARY 9–18

This person is ruled by Uranus and Venus, which gives him tremendous charisma and a magnetic attraction. Although he still has the characteristic Aquarian distance and emotional reserve, he's warm, charming, and funny. He is also very idealistic, with high expectations of his partner.

PISCES
FEBRUARY 19–MARCH 20

Ruling planet	Neptune
Element	Water
Symbol	Fish
Gemstone	Amethyst
Day of the week	Thursday
Area of the body	Feet
Classic characteristics	Sensitive, emotional, empathic, altruistic, escapist, compassionate, selfless, weak-willed, secretive

A Piscean is kind, loving, and considerate, with a powerful sense of compassion. Sometimes it's as though she's got a layer of skin missing. Dealing with harsh reality is a challenge for her because she would much rather escape from any unpleasantness into a world of her own. She needs to find positive outlets for her considerable imagination and creativity.

These are some of the general characteristics of Pisces. However, the sign is divided into three sub-sections, each of which adds a different layer to typical Piscean traits.

PISCES BORN FEBRUARY 19–28

With her double rulership by Neptune, this Piscean can sometimes struggle to keep her feet on the ground. Highly sensitive, empathic, and affectionate, it's almost impossible for her to contain her strong emotions. She's a born romantic too, with a tendency to idealize partners. She has a tremendous affinity with animals.

PISCES BORN FEBRUARY 29–MARCH 9

This Piscean is ruled by Neptune and the Moon, which makes her much more domesticated and practical than other members of this sign. She needs a happy home life and enjoys taking care of her loved ones, even if it's on a shoestring. She can be moody, despite not recognizing this trait in herself, and is very sensitive to the atmosphere around her.

PISCES BORN MARCH 10–20

Ruled by Neptune and Pluto, this Piscean is much tougher emotionally than other members of her sign. She has a stronger view of reality and a clever ability to make money from her many talents. She is capable of great emotional depth and intensity but can sometimes be carried away by her feelings.

LIVING BY THE MOON

Of all the planets in the sky, the Moon holds the most mystique. The Sun rises and sets each day but it always looks the same. The Moon, on the other hand, goes through a monthly cycle that is very noticeable, even to people who aren't interested in astronomy.

Astrologically, the Moon also exerts a strong influence over our day-to-day lives, so it can be very helpful to track the lunar cycle each month. For instance, the Moon rules our behavior, our habits, our maternal feelings, our attitude toward food, our moods, and our instinctive emotions. For Cancerians, the Moon (which rules their sign) is a particularly important planet, but it plays an essential role in all our lives.

THE MOON IN THE SIGNS

From our vantage point on Earth, the Moon spends two-and-a-half days in each sign of the zodiac. Each sign influences the Moon in a particular way, so it makes sense to capitalize on this by planning a specific activity for a day when the Moon is in a sign that is beneficial for that activity. For instance, Gemini rules communication, so days when the Moon is in Gemini are great for writing letters, making phone calls or buying equipment that helps you to connect with the rest of the world.

There are many internet sites and books that will tell you which sign the Moon occupies on a particular day, and you can then plan your activities accordingly. Here are some suggestions:

If you are familiar with your own chart, you can track the Moon's monthly journey through it, noting how you feel when the Moon returns to the degree and sign that it occupied at the time of your birth. You may be more emotional than usual or feel very receptive to the atmosphere around you.

The Moon is clearly visible in the sky so it's easy to track its monthly cycle.

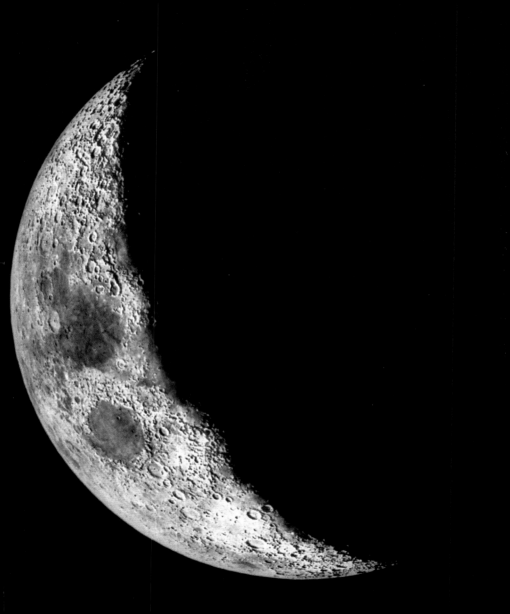

MOON IN ARIES

A good time for concentrating on personal projects and activities, for standing up for yourself, taking the lead, engaging in competitive sports or adopting a pioneering, adventurous spirit.

MOON IN TAURUS

Good for activities connected with material and physical security, such as buying a house. It's also good for being close to nature and for activities that have a grounding effect.

MOON IN GEMINI

Excellent for all forms of communication, such as chatting to friends or writing letters. It's also a favorable time for making contact with neighbors and close relatives.

MOON IN CANCER

Lovely for enjoying your home comforts and other activities that give you emotional security and satisfaction. It's ideal for entertaining close friends and family at home.

MOON IN LEO

This is perfect for any activities that allow you to express your true self, especially if they put you in the limelight. It's also good for celebrations, social events, and being with your favorite people.

MOON IN VIRGO

The ideal time for activities that require a careful, detailed, and analytical approach. It's also excellent for matters connected with your work, your health, and your pets.

MOON IN LIBRA

This is a time when you can concentrate on your relationships, aiming to introduce as much balance and harmony as possible. You may prefer to be with others than to be by yourself.

MOON IN SCORPIO

This is a great opportunity to focus on your deepest feelings and to discuss them with people you trust. It's a time of intense emotions so you need to guard against jealousy or suspicion.

MOON IN SAGITTARIUS

A good time for activities connected with philosophy, spirituality, religion, and education. It's also great for seizing opportunities and rising to challenges.

MOON IN CAPRICORN

This is excellent for activities that will boost your reputation, command respect, or advance your long-term plans. Watch out for a tendency to work too hard or to take life too seriously.

MOON IN AQUARIUS

A time for expressing your individuality and independence. It's good for activities connected with science and technology, such as buying a computer, and for humanitarian concerns.

MOON IN PISCES

This is marvelous for using your imagination and intuition, and for bringing out your psychic gifts. It's a good time for activities connected with charities, philanthropy, and compassion.

THE MOON'S CYCLE

In addition to noting the sign that the Moon is occupying each day, it's also worthwhile paying attention to New and Full Moons. At the time of a New Moon, the Moon has vanished from the sky completely, which is why it's referred to as "the dark of the Moon." Although we often think of a New Moon as being a tiny crescent, in fact it's ceased to be a New Moon by the time it becomes visible. Fourteen days later, at the time of a Full Moon, the Moon is a perfect circle in the sky.

New Moon

When there is a New Moon, the Sun and Moon occupy the same zodiac sign. Astrologers believe that New Moons are times of beginnings. It's always a good idea to initiate new projects and to launch fresh ideas at the time of a New Moon. However, you should try to allow at least six hours to elapse after the New Moon is exact before putting your plans into practice. If your diary doesn't give you the exact time of the New Moon, there are many Web sites that will. There is a New Moon every 29½ days.

Full Moon

At the time of a Full Moon, the Sun and Moon are separated by 180 degrees. Therefore, they are in opposite signs. For instance, if the Sun is in Libra and the Moon is in Aries, astrologers say that there is a Full Moon in Aries.

A Full Moon is a time for endings. A lunar cycle has ended and therefore we should complete tasks and other projects in our lives. It's a very good opportunity to tidy up loose ends and to sort out problems. As with New Moons, you should allow at least six hours to elapse after the exact Full Moon before taking action. There is a Full Moon every 29½ days.

Eclipses

There are several occasions each year when a New or Full Moon is said to be eclipsed. This means that the Earth's shadow has fallen across it. Eclipses are extremely important lunar events because they carry extra power. If there is an eclipse on your birthday or one day either side of it, you can be sure that your coming 12 months will be highly significant, with major changes in store.

The Full Moon sometimes looks orange. This is because it's illuminating a lot of pollution in the atmosphere.

THE PLANETS

The planets in our solar system have a tremendous effect on our lives. Each planet (and the Sun and Moon come into this category in Western astrology, even though astrologers know full well that they are a sun and a satellite respectively) exerts its own influence over us and this is reflected in our birth charts.

There have been many theories about how the planets' activities mirror our own lives. Some people believe that the planets exert some form of gravitational pull over us. Others simply accept that there is a correlation between the planets and our lives that has yet to be explained. What really happens doesn't matter. What is important is that it works.

THE TRADITIONAL PLANETS

In astrology, the planets are divided into groups. The seven traditional planets, which are all visible to the naked eye and were all that we knew of the solar system until the 1780s, are the Sun, Moon, Mercury, Venus, Mars, Jupiter, and Saturn. The Sun describes an essential part of ourselves. The Moon determines what is familiar to us, as well as our habits and instinctive reactions. Mercury rules the way we communicate with others. Venus describes what we like and what we yearn for. Mars describes our drive, aggression, and survival instincts. Jupiter rules expansion and growth, both literally and metaphorically. Saturn, on the other hand, rules limitation, rules, and boundaries.

THE MODERN PLANETS

The final three planets (to date) in our solar system are Uranus, Neptune, and Pluto, and they have only been known relatively recently. Uranus was discovered in 1781, Neptune in 1846, and Pluto in 1930. Uranus rules disruption, revolution, and radical change. Neptune rules confusion, compassion, and transcendence. Pluto rules transition, deep psychological change, and whatever we consider to be taboo.

We all have these ten planets in our birth charts, which means we all express the essence of these planets according to the signs in which they fall. For instance, someone born with Mercury in Gemini (very lively and chatty) will communicate in an entirely different way from someone with Mercury in Capricorn (someone who likes to discuss serious topics).

Mercury and Venus are the two planets closest to the Earth. Pluto is the most distant.

PLANETARY CYCLES

Although it is beyond the scope of this book to give you detailed information about the position of each of the ten planets when you were born, there are many Web sites that will provide you with a copy of your birth chart. Alternatively, you can consult an astrologer who will draw up your chart and also explain it to you.

Even without this basic astrological information you can still become aware of the effect of the cycles of the planets in your life. Each planet takes a particular length of time to return to the position it occupied at the time of your birth, and along the way it reaches several points at which it is a set number of degrees from its natal position. It is at these points, known as aspects, where it activates the natal position and highlights the role it plays in your life. The slower a planet moves, the more powerful its impact when it makes an aspect to its natal position. Here are two examples:

JUPITER CYCLES
Jupiter, the planet of good fortune, expansion, and knowledge, has a cycle of just under 12 years. This means that it returns to its natal position shortly before

Jupiter is twice as large as all the other planets in the solar system combined.

our 12th birthday, then again when we are nearly 24, and so on. Each Jupiter cycle is a time of expansion and exploration, when things go well for us.

SATURN CYCLES

Saturn, the planet of experience, limitation, and structure, has a cycle of 29 years. Whenever it aspects its natal position we discover Saturn's lessons about learning from experience. We first feel its impact at the age of seven, when it makes a square

The restriction and structure associated with Saturn are represented by its ice rings.

aspect to its natal position, and again at 14, when it opposes its natal position, then again at 21 when it once again squares its natal position. Our first Saturn return, at the age of 29, is always an important time of growing up, when we face our responsibilities. The cycle then begins again. Our second Saturn return coincides with our fifth Jupiter return.

PART THREE

Chinese astrology

HOW CHINESE ASTROLOGY WORKS

Chinese astrology divides our personalities into 12 signs, all of which are ruled by animals. This is a tradition that started several millennia ago.

In fact, legend has it that Chinese astrology originated when the dying Buddha summoned 12 different animals to visit him, and thanked them by giving each one its own year in the Chinese zodiac. The names of the animals can vary slightly.

THE LUNAR CALENDAR

Chinese astrology is centered on the lunar calendar, unlike Western astrology which is based on the movement of the Sun. Lunar months are shorter than solar months and, as a result, the Chinese New Year starts on a different day each year, at some point between mid-January and mid-February. That's because the Chinese New Year always coincides with the New Moon in Aquarius, as it is known in the West.

DISCOVERING YOUR ANIMAL SIGN

The first step in Chinese astrology is to discover which is your animal sign. This depends on the year in which you were born, and the chart on pages 60–61 gives the animal sign for each year from 1900 to 2019. If you were born at any time between mid-February and the following mid-January, you can safely assume that you belong to the animal sign that's listed in the chart under your year of birth. However, if you were born between mid-January and mid-February, you should turn to the relevant animal sign and check the dates for the year in question. You may find that you belong to the previous animal sign or the next one.

For instance, if you were born on February 17, 1958, you might think that you belong to the sign of the Dog, but if you turn to that sign (see pages 82–83) you'll see that the Dog year doesn't actually begin until February 19, 1958, so you were actually born under the sign of the Rooster.

THE ELEMENTS

Chinese astrology recognizes five elements: Metal, Water, Wood, Fire, and Earth. You may imagine that Air should be one of them, to correlate with Western astrology, but the Chinese believe that Air is the life force itself and is therefore too important to be called an element.

Each year is assigned a different element, so you can refine the meaning of your Chinese sign by discovering which element you belong to according to your year of birth. For instance, a birth date of February 17, 1958 means that you are a Fire Rooster. This means that you still have all the classic Rooster characteristics but that they are influenced by the element of fire. The elemental cycle of Chinese signs repeats itself every 60 years, which means that the next year of the Fire Rooster is 2017.

THE FUTURE

You can discover what the future holds for your Chinese sign by discovering how it fares in each of the 12 animal years, and this information is contained on pages 86–97. If you aren't sure which year belongs to which animal sign, the table on pages 60–61 will remind you. Under this system not only can you glimpse the future, but also look up memorable years in the past to see whether they correlate with what Chinese astrology tells you.

COMPATIBILITY

Some Chinese signs get on well together, while others have more difficulties in establishing harmony. The compatibility wheel shows which signs get on best with each other because they have so much in common. Therefore, the Rat has the greatest affinity with the Dragon and Monkey; the Ox with the Snake and the Rooster; the Tiger with the Horse and the Dog; and the Rabbit with the Sheep and the Pig. Traditionally, signs that oppose each other on this wheel, such as the Dragon and the Dog, have difficulties in understanding one another and do not get along well.

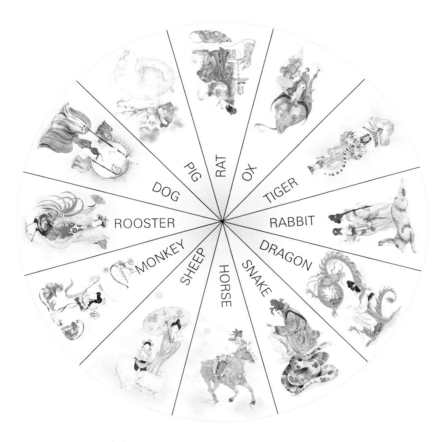

Use this wheel to see which signs are most compatible, and which are in opposition to each other.

THE ANIMAL YEARS AT A GLANCE

Here is the complete chart of Chinese signs from 1900 until 2019. You can use it as a quick way to discover someone's animal sign, and then turn to the relevant page to find out more about his personality based on his particular element.

For instance, if you want to know more about a friend who was born in 1947, you can start off by consulting this chart. You will see that he was born in the year of the Pig. You can then turn to the Pig pages to read about the general characteristics of his sign, and also to discover which element he belongs to (it is the Fire element). If someone is born in January or February, don't forget to check his date of birth against the dates given for his animal year to ensure that you know which is his Chinese sign. This is a chart for all the years of the 20th century and some of the 21st century. However, you can easily work backward to discover the animal sign of someone born in the 19th century.

DETERMINE YOUR CHINESE ASTROLOGICAL SIGN

Use this chart to determine your own or somone else's animal sign by looking-up the year of birth.

Animal	Year									
Rat	1900	1912	1924	1936	1948	1960	1972	1984	1996	2008
Ox	1901	1913	1925	1937	1949	1961	1973	1985	1997	2009
Tiger	1902	1914	1926	1938	1950	1962	1974	1986	1998	2010
Rabbit	1903	1915	1927	1939	1951	1963	1975	1987	1999	2011
Dragon	1904	1916	1928	1940	1952	1964	1976	1988	2000	2012
Snake	1905	1917	1929	1941	1953	1965	1977	1989	2001	2013
Horse	1906	1918	1930	1942	1954	1966	1978	1990	2002	2014
Sheep	1907	1919	1931	1943	1955	1967	1979	1991	2003	2015
Monkey	1908	1920	1932	1944	1956	1968	1980	1992	2004	2016
Rooster	1909	1921	1933	1945	1957	1969	1981	1993	2005	2017
Dog	1910	1922	1934	1946	1958	1970	1982	1994	2006	2018
Pig	1911	1923	1935	1947	1959	1971	1983	1995	2007	2019

THE RAT

Bright, lively, and gregarious, the Rat is an entertaining companion with a great sense of humor. He has a lifelong thirst for knowledge and is always busy with his latest interests.

THE METAL RAT

JANUARY 31, 1900–FEBRUARY 18, 1901
JANUARY 28, 1960–FEBRUARY 14, 1961

Competitive and ambitious, the Metal Rat knows exactly what he wants out of life and he'll work hard until he gets it. Family life may have to go by the wayside because he is so focused on his goals. He may cultivate people for materialistic reasons.

THE WATER RAT

FEBRUARY 18, 1912–FEBRUARY 5, 1913
FEBRUARY 15, 1972–FEBRUARY 2, 1973

The Water Rat is charming, diplomatic and friendly—qualities which help to make him deservedly popular. He enjoys travel and needs frequent changes of scene. Rather idealistic, he can sometimes be deceived by people. He needs a supportive and loving partner.

THE WOOD RAT

FEBRUARY 5, 1924–JANUARY 24, 1925
FEBRUARY 2, 1984–FEBRUARY 19, 1985

Although this person may give the impression of being carefree, secretly he is much more sensitive and anxious than he lets on. He needs plenty of encouragement to combat his insecurities. His sense of humor is his greatest ally.

THE FIRE RAT

JANUARY 24, 1936–FEBRUARY 10, 1937
FEBRUARY 19, 1996–FEBRUARY 6, 1997

The Fire Rat is impatient, energetic, and independent, and therefore enjoys meeting challenges head-on. He's honest and loyal, and expects his friends to behave in the same way. He has a good knack for making and keeping money.

THE EARTH RAT

FEBRUARY 10, 1948–JANUARY 28, 1949
FEBRUARY 7, 2008–JANUARY 25, 2009

Practical, resourceful and a traditionalist, the Earth Rat usually succeeds in his ambition to do well in life. He likes others to have a good opinion of him, although he can be quite critical in return. He is affectionate, sociable, and friendly.

THE OX

Strong, sure, and opinionated, the Ox is dependable and stoical. No stranger to hard work, the Ox always does her best and is very reliable. She is trustworthy, sensible, and practical.

THE METAL OX

FEBRUARY 19, 1901–FEBRUARY 7, 1902
FEBRUARY 15, 1961–FEBRUARY 4, 1962

You can always rely on a Metal Ox in a crisis, even though she may tell you off for getting into this state in the first place. She has strong opinions which she likes to share with others, and finds it hard to accept that people may not agree with her.

THE WATER OX

FEBRUARY 6, 1913–JANUARY 25, 1914
FEBRUARY 3, 1973–JANUARY 22, 1974

This person is a skilled organizer, but prefers to do things her own way rather than anyone else's. Once she's motivated she likes to act quickly. She's loving and family-minded, but easily bears grudges if she feels that people have let her down.

THE WOOD OX

JANUARY 25, 1925–FEBRUARY 12, 1926
FEBRUARY 20, 1985–FEBRUARY 8, 1986

A born survivor, the Wood Ox always bounces back from adversity, even if it's through sheer grit and determination. She is highly motivated and must always have a project on the go. She likes to get her own way and will devise many tactics to ensure that this happens.

THE FIRE OX

FEBRUARY 11, 1937–JANUARY 30, 1938
FEBRUARY 7, 1997–JANUARY 27, 1998

Active and impatient, a Fire Ox makes no bones about getting what she wants and will work hard to achieve her goals. As a result, she can lack subtlety and patience. She's affectionate and sociable but chooses her friends carefully.

THE EARTH OX

JANUARY 29, 1949–FEBRUARY 16, 1950
JANUARY 26, 2009–FEBRUARY 13, 2010

The Earth Ox has a chequered emotional life because she's quite naïve, insecure, and can be too trusting. As a result, she's skilled at letting others cry on her shoulder because she knows exactly what they've been through. She is practical, logical, responsible, and a perfectionist.

THE TIGER

The Tiger always wants to look good and takes a lot of trouble over his appearance. A Tiger also enjoys the excitement of traveling at speed. Emotional independence is important to him.

THE WATER TIGER

FEBRUARY 8, 1902–JANUARY 27, 1903
FEBRUARY 5, 1962–JANUARY 24, 1963

Business-minded and ambitious, the Water Tiger knows where he's going in life. He likes to bask in the limelight, regardless of the career he chooses, and has a powerfully creative imagination which he needs to express. He has a short fuse.

THE WOOD TIGER

JANUARY 26, 1914–FEBRUARY 13, 1915
JANUARY 23, 1974–FEBRUARY 10, 1975

The Wood Tiger is very versatile and needs a career that brings him plenty of change and mental stimulation. He's witty, lively, and great company, so is deservedly popular. Despite a strong romantic streak, he hates to be tied down emotionally.

THE FIRE TIGER

FEBRUARY 13, 1926–FEBRUARY 1, 1927
FEBRUARY 9, 1986–JANUARY 28, 1987

This person's career comes before any emotional ties, so he may concentrate on establishing a name for himself before settling down. He works tirelessly, and his magnetic charm opens many doors for him. It's almost impossible for him to listen to criticism of his actions.

THE EARTH TIGER

JANUARY 31, 1938–FEBRUARY 18, 1939
JANUARY 28, 1998–FEBRUARY 15, 1999

The Earth Tiger is a born leader who likes to tackle one task at a time. Although he's good at giving advice, he doesn't like taking it and prefers to follow his own path through life, never admitting that he may have made mistakes. He's loving, passionate, and can be jealous.

THE METAL TIGER

FEBRUARY 17, 1950–FEBRUARY 5, 1951
FEBRUARY 14, 2010–FEBRUARY 2, 2011

The Metal Tiger loves outflanking the competition and coming first. He is very sure of himself, with a hunger for success and a conviction that nothing less will do. It's difficult for him to reveal his true feelings, preferring to hide them behind a socially acceptable mask.

THE RABBIT

The Rabbit needs comfort, luxury and order in order to feel happy. This sign is the clothes horse of the Chinese zodiac, and both sexes believe that it's important to make the best of themselves. The Rabbit is a true survivor, partly because she remains optimistic about the future, come what may.

THE WATER RABBIT

JANUARY 28, 1903–FEBRUARY 15, 1904
JANUARY 25, 1963–FEBRUARY 12, 1964

Home, family and friends are essential ingredients for the Water Rabbit. This person is sensitive, kind, and affectionate, and often needs to be treated gently by others. She must find productive outlets for her intuition and artistic abilities.

THE WOOD RABBIT

FEBRUARY 14, 1915–FEBRUARY 2, 1916
FEBRUARY 11, 1975–JANUARY 30, 1976

The Wood Rabbit doesn't like disruption, no matter from which direction it comes. Instead, she needs peace and quiet, and a loving home life. Kind and considerate, she likes to take care of others. Although she's friendly and affectionate, she lacks any sort of romantic impulse.

THE FIRE RABBIT

FEBRUARY 2, 1927–JANUARY 22, 1928
JANUARY 29, 1987–FEBRUARY 17, 1988

The Fire Rabbit needs a career that offers her plenty of scope for challenges and success. However, she finds it difficult to cope with too much tension as it makes her moody and can also compromise her health. She can be self-centered in emotional matters.

THE EARTH RABBIT

FEBRUARY 19, 1939–FEBRUARY 7, 1940
FEBRUARY 16, 1999–FEBRUARY 4, 2000

Hard-working and industrious, the Earth Rabbit has good business flair and is an excellent colleague. However, a liking for speaking her mind, regardless of other people's feelings, can cause problems. She needs a strong, committed partnership in order to feel secure.

THE METAL RABBIT

FEBRUARY 6, 1951–JANUARY 26, 1952
FEBRUARY 3, 2011–JANUARY 22, 2012

Reliable and trustworthy, the Metal Rabbit is as good as her word. She's ambitious and gifted, but has a tendency to trip herself up by taking herself too seriously. She can become quite melancholic at times. She has a small circle of loyal friends.

THE DRAGON

The Dragon believes in speaking his mind, regardless of the consequences. He isn't deliberately setting out to shock others, he is simply being true to himself and saying what he thinks. Despite this, the Dragon is a very popular member of the Chinese zodiac.

THE WOOD DRAGON

FEBRUARY 16, 1904–FEBRUARY 3, 1905
FEBRUARY 13, 1964–FEBRUARY 1, 1965

Responsible and reliable, the Wood Dragon is a great source of comfort to his friends and family. He has much more tact than other Dragons and this helps him to make progress at work. He thinks seriously about life but is a very lively conversationalist.

THE FIRE DRAGON

FEBRUARY 3, 1916–JANUARY 22, 1917
JANUARY 31, 1976–FEBRUARY 17, 1977

The Fire Dragon is eccentric and outspoken, with a tendency to find fault in others. He does better working by himself than in a group. Nevertheless, he's loving and supportive toward his family and friends. He adores spending money!

THE METAL DRAGON

FEBRUARY 8, 1940–JANUARY 26, 1941
FEBRUARY 5, 2000–JANUARY 23, 2001

The Metal Dragon is ambitious and hard-working, whether in his career or his private life. He has a tendency to brood and to become possessive. He is just as likely to marry for materialistic reasons as for love because he needs the security and status that financial success brings.

THE EARTH DRAGON

JANUARY 23, 1928–FEBRUARY 9, 1929
FEBRUARY 18, 1988–FEBRUARY 5, 1989

Although money isn't the motivating factor for him that it is for some Dragons, the Earth Dragon still has a knack for accruing great wealth through the sweat of his brow. He needs a career that allows him to shine and to express his flamboyant and exciting personality.

THE WATER DRAGON

JANUARY 27, 1952–FEBRUARY 13, 1953
JANUARY 23, 2012–FEBRUARY 9, 2013

This person is dynamic company, because he's witty, clever, and entertaining. He is also a very loyal friend who takes great interest in the welfare of the people he cares about. He's good at seizing opportunities and making the most of whatever life brings his way.

THE SNAKE

One of the most attractive of the animal signs, the Snake takes great trouble with her appearance. Although she seems calm and collected, inside she can be nervy and unsure of herself.

THE WOOD SNAKE

FEBRUARY 4, 1905–JANUARY 23, 1906
FEBRUARY 2, 1965–JANUARY 21, 1966

The Wood Snake is a skilled communicator and may well make a successful profession out of this talent. She's fascinated by the mysterious side of life. She has a tendency to be over-emotional and jealous of partners, with a dislike of too much of her own company.

THE FIRE SNAKE

JANUARY 23, 1917–FEBRUARY 10, 1918
FEBRUARY 18, 1977–FEBRUARY 6, 1978

It's important for a Fire Snake to have a good reputation and to earn the respect of others. She enjoys travel and has strong ambitions, especially in a career that will put her in the public eye. She is loving and supportive of partners.

THE EARTH SNAKE

FEBRUARY 10, 1929–JANUARY 29, 1930
FEBRUARY 6, 1989–JANUARY 26, 1990

The Earth Snake is calm and stable. She enjoys being presented with a challenge and always does her best to come out on top. She works hard and has great organizational skills. She loves to spend money on luxuries, and needs a comfortable, stable, and secure home.

THE METAL SNAKE

JANUARY 27, 1941–FEBRUARY 14, 1942
JANUARY 24, 2001–FEBRUARY 11, 2002

This person has a strong need for security —emotionally, physically, and materially. Being shy, she gives the impression of being reserved and withdrawn but opens up to people she trusts. Sadly, sometimes she tends to trust the wrong people.

THE WATER SNAKE

FEBRUARY 14, 1953–FEBRUARY 2, 1954
FEBRUARY 10, 2013–JANUARY 30, 2014

Reserved, intelligent, and serious, the Water Snake has a strong code of honor. She enjoys specializing in a particular subject so she can become an expert on it. A deep thinker, she's intrigued by life's mysteries and may be drawn to psychic matters.

THE HORSE

Lively and always fascinated by life, the Horse is an entertaining companion who strives to get as much out of every day as possible. He enjoys being spontaneous and is a free spirit at heart.

THE FIRE HORSE

JANUARY 24, 1906–FEBRUARY 11, 1907
JANUARY 22, 1966–FEBRUARY 8, 1967

Clever, sporty, and restless, the Fire Horse can find it hard to settle down because he likes to keep on the move. Despite this and a reluctance to reveal his true feelings, he's very popular because he is so affectionate, witty, and entertaining.

THE EARTH HORSE

FEBRUARY 11, 1918–JANUARY 30, 1919
FEBRUARY 7, 1978–JANUARY 27, 1979

The Earth Horse is so focused on making a good living in order to accumulate some financial security that his home life may suffer. Nevertheless, he excels at being self-employed. His friends and family mean the world to him but he's much less interested in people outside this inner circle.

THE WATER HORSE

FEBRUARY 15, 1942–FEBRUARY 4, 1943
FEBRUARY 12, 2002–JANUARY 31, 2003

Restless, with a preference for keeping on the move, the Water Horse needs a life that is full of surprises and change. As a result, it can be difficult for him to form committed relationships so he needs partners who are adaptable and who know how to keep him amused.

THE METAL HORSE

JANUARY 30, 1930–FEBRUARY 16, 1931
JANUARY 27, 1990–FEBRUARY 14, 1991

This person excels in business matters because he likes the status and money that come with success. However, he's impatient and can struggle with tedious routine. He's popular and friendly, but finds it difficult to express his emotions because he is frightened of being hurt.

THE WOOD HORSE

FEBRUARY 3, 1954–JANUARY 23, 1955
JANUARY 31, 2014–FEBRUARY 18, 2015

The Wood Horse is often happier as a friend than a partner, and can find it hard to form permanent relationships. He enjoys being in the countryside rather than the town. He's a hard worker, possibly even a workaholic, who always needs to take the lead and be in charge.

THE SHEEP

Despite outward appearances, the Sheep is very sensitive, affectionate, and vulnerable, and her feelings are easily hurt. She needs people in her life that she can trust.

THE FIRE SHEEP

FEBRUARY 12, 1907–FEBRUARY 1, 1908
FEBRUARY 9, 1967–JANUARY 28, 1968

Money can cause worries for the Fire Sheep because she is so good at spending it but so poor at budgeting for it. She is volatile and moody, and easily deterred from her goals when problems arise. Nevertheless, she is fascinating company because she has such wide-ranging interests.

THE EARTH SHEEP

JANUARY 31, 1919–FEBRUARY 18, 1920
JANUARY 28, 1979–FEBRUARY 15, 1980

The Earth Sheep doesn't like being told what to do, even when it's necessary. She prefers to go her own way, especially at work. Relationships can suffer because of her lack of tact. She struggles to manage her finances because she enjoys spending money so much.

THE METAL SHEEP

FEBRUARY 17, 1931–FEBRUARY 6, 1932
FEBRUARY 15, 1991–FEBRUARY 3, 1992

The Metal Sheep likes to take her time and won't let herself be rushed into doing anything before she is ready. Cautious and thrifty, she likes to set aside money for a rainy day. She excels at making emotional connections with others and tuning into them on a deep level.

THE WATER SHEEP

FEBRUARY 5, 1943–JANUARY 24, 1944
FEBRUARY 1, 2003–JANUARY 21, 2004

The Water Sheep finds it easy to communicate with others and may have tremendous writing skills. It's hard for her to cope with change because she has such a strong need for security, even though she may give a very different impression to the world outside.

THE WOOD SHEEP

JANUARY 24, 1955–FEBRUARY 11, 1956
FEBRUARY 19, 2015–FEBRUARY 8, 2016

The Wood Sheep is kind, sweet-natured, and affectionate. She is a people-pleaser with an instinctive ability to get on well with others. She's warm, loving, and cheerful, although this outer persona can mask moody and depressive tendencies. She has a particular affinity for music.

THE MONKEY

The Monkey's life must be full of drama and activity, otherwise he gets bored. Tales of his exploits help to keep his many friends amused, although sometimes he embroiders the facts to make them sound more entertaining. He is witty and great company.

THE EARTH MONKEY

FEBRUARY 2, 1908–JANUARY 21, 1909
JANUARY 29, 1968–FEBRUARY 16, 1969

Change presents problems for the Earth Monkey, who values his steady routine. As a result, he likes to take charge of situations and is great at motivating himself, especially at work. He has a perfectionist streak and expects great things from his partners.

THE METAL MONKEY

FEBRUARY 19, 1920–FEBRUARY 7, 1921
FEBRUARY 16, 1980–FEBRUARY 4, 1981

The Metal Monkey is a hard worker but prefers to be left to his own devices, and so he isn't good at being part of a team. He has a tendency to be a workaholic, at the cost of his personal life. When seeking a partner, he should look for one who understands his need for freedom and independence.

THE WOOD MONKEY

JANUARY 25, 1944–FEBRUARY 12, 1945
JANUARY 22, 2004–FEBRUARY 8, 2005

Creative and inventive, the Wood Monkey needs plenty of outlets for his many talents. He is fascinated by life and loves learning new topics. Affectionate, loyal, and friendly, he often allows his partners to gain the upper hand and can therefore struggle to maintain long-term relationships.

THE WATER MONKEY

FEBRUARY 7, 1932–JANUARY 25, 1933
FEBRUARY 4, 1992–JANUARY 22, 1993

Versatile, restless, and clever, the Water Monkey enjoys changes and challenges. He finds it easy to get on well with others, thanks to his sharp wit and ability to be affectionate. However, his innate sensitivity makes him overly anxious about upsetting other people.

THE FIRE MONKEY

FEBRUARY 12, 1956–JANUARY 30, 1957
FEBRUARY 9, 2016–JANUARY 27, 2017

Always busy, the Fire Monkey lives life to the full, trying to gain the maximum from every moment. As a result it can be difficult for him to relax. He loves analyzing situations and people, but expects everyone to agree with his conclusions. He excels at taking the lead.

THE ROOSTER

Honest to the point of bluntness, the Rooster enjoys sharing her thoughts with everyone around her. She has a tremendous store of knowledge which always stands her in good stead. She usually has a scheme or project on the go, and if it fails she will quickly devise another one.

THE EARTH ROOSTER

JANUARY 22, 1909–FEBRUARY 9, 1910
FEBRUARY 17, 1969–FEBRUARY 5, 1970

Determined and steadfast, the Earth Rooster knows what she wants out of life and makes sure that she gets it sooner or later. She's a hard worker, excelling at details and organization. She is loving and friendly but finds it difficult to be demonstrative, even with her nearest and dearest.

THE METAL ROOSTER

FEBRUARY 8, 1921–JANUARY 27, 1922
FEBRUARY 5, 1981–JANUARY 24, 1982

The Metal Rooster loves tidiness and order in all areas of her life. Competitive and ambitious, she excels at any work connected with charities, politics, and the media. She is loyal and friendly but her brutal honesty can hurt the feelings of partners, family, and friends.

THE WOOD ROOSTER

FEBRUARY 13, 1945–FEBRUARY 1, 1946
FEBRUARY 9, 2005–JANUARY 28, 2006

Considerate, cheerful, and warm-hearted, the Wood Rooster likes to be with other people and needs to know that she's loved. She enjoys switching from one project to another but needs to learn to concentrate on one thing at a time. She remains youthful throughout her life.

THE WATER ROOSTER

JANUARY 26, 1933–FEBRUARY 13, 1934
JANUARY 23, 1993–FEBRUARY 9, 1994

Despite an innate sense of insecurity, the Water Rooster will work hard to reach the top rung of life's ladder. She has a tendency to worry, but her tremendous sense of humor helps her to keep problems in perspective. She needs to have people around her.

THE FIRE ROOSTER

JANUARY 31, 1957–FEBRUARY 18, 1958
JANUARY 28, 2017–FEBRUARY 15, 2018

Strong-willed and forceful, the Fire Rooster has no difficulty in making an impact on others. She is clever, quick-witted, and perennially optimistic, which makes her popular with her many friends. Despite this, she often feels lonely and emotionally cut off from the people around her.

THE DOG

Gentle and sensitive, the Dog is kind-hearted and considerate. He is trusting and honest, and expects the same behavior from everyone else. He likes to support others and wants them to be happy, but isn't so good at protecting his own interests.

THE METAL DOG

FEBRUARY 10, 1910–JANUARY 29, 1911
FEBRUARY 6, 1970–JANUARY 26, 1971

A good leader, the Metal Dog is organized and efficient. He has dogged determination and will work hard until he achieves his aims, at which point he will expect people to congratulate him. Relationships can be difficult for this person because he's critical, obstinate, and outspoken.

THE WATER DOG

JANUARY 28, 1922–FEBRUARY 15, 1923
JANUARY 25, 1982–FEBRUARY 12, 1983

Although the Water Dog appears confident, inside he lacks confidence in his own abilities, with a tendency toward pessimism. He is sensitive but shy, which gives him a somewhat aloof and withdrawn persona. He's a sterling friend who is always happy to help others.

THE FIRE DOG

FEBRUARY 2, 1946–JANUARY 21, 1947
JANUARY 29, 2006–FEBRUARY 17, 2007

Still waters run deep for the friendly Fire Dog, making him prone to bouts of depression and moodiness when things aren't going well. He is very protective of partners, with a tendency to smother-love whenever he feels insecure. Even so, he is charming, intelligent, and entertaining.

THE WOOD DOG

FEBRUARY 14, 1934–FEBRUARY 3, 1935
FEBRUARY 10, 1994–JANUARY 30, 1995

The Wood Dog loves his creature comforts and is usually happiest when at home. He enjoys being surrounded by nature and has an affinity for plants. He's loyal, affectionate, and charming, but can sometimes be a bag of nerves beneath a calm exterior.

THE EARTH DOG

FEBRUARY 19, 1958–FEBRUARY 7, 1959
FEBRUARY 16, 2018–FEBRUARY 4, 2019

Despite wanting to do well in life, the Earth Dog puts his family and relationships above all else. It's hard for him to trust people and as a result he can be bossy with them. He's good at making money. Tension can get the better of him, leading to comfort eating.

THE PIG

Kind-hearted and considerate, the Pig is one of the most loving and devoted Chinese signs. The Pig likes to help others, with no thought for what she might receive in return. It's hard for her to face unpleasant facts and harsh reality, so she can be escapist at times.

THE METAL PIG

JANUARY 30, 1911–FEBRUARY 17, 1912
JANUARY 27, 1971–FEBRUARY 14, 1972

Charming and trustworthy, the Metal Pig has moderate ambitions. She is more interested in having happy relationships than in being wildly successful in the wider world. She has a healthy ego but can sometimes become too pleased with herself.

THE WATER PIG

FEBRUARY 16, 1923–FEBRUARY 4, 1924
FEBRUARY 13, 1983–FEBRUARY 1, 1984

Diplomatic, affectionate, and friendly, the Water Pig is justifiably popular. She likes to be with people she knows inside and out, and is also very fond of children and animals. She's canny with money, knowing how to make it stretch as far as possible without ever becoming parsimonious.

THE FIRE PIG

JANUARY 22, 1947–FEBRUARY 9, 1948
FEBRUARY 18, 2007–FEBRUARY 6, 2008

Confident and self-assured, the Fire Pig seems to breeze through life. She's quick to fight injustice and has many causes that are dear to her heart. Great company, she is amusing, funny, and warm-hearted. She has many friends but her family will always come first.

THE WOOD PIG

FEBRUARY 4, 1935–JANUARY 23, 1936
JANUARY 31, 1995–FEBRUARY 18, 1996

Witty and articulate, the Wood Pig does well in life. It's hard for her to refuse people's requests for help, and as a result she can stretch herself to breaking point. She's so sensitive that she's always worried about upsetting others, yet she finds it hard to show her true feelings.

THE EARTH PIG

FEBRUARY 8, 1959–JANUARY 27, 1960
FEBRUARY 5, 2019–JANUARY 24, 2020

Practical, easy-going, and even-tempered, the Earth Pig is a tower of strength. She works hard, whether for herself or for other people. Her innocence and ability to see the best in others means she can sometimes be taken for a ride. She's interested in food but must watch her weight.

THE FUTURE FOR THE RAT

Here is a brief summary of what the Rat can expect in the following animal years:

Year of the Rat	Great for enterprise and making the most of opportunities.
Year of the Ox	A responsible time. Family matters bring happiness.
Year of the Tiger	Travel is a possibility. Be very careful with money.
Year of the Rabbit	Good for business contacts and increasing your family circle.
Year of the Dragon	Success and happiness in your career and love life.
Year of the Snake	After a difficult start financially, things begin to improve.
Year of the Horse	Avoid taking unnecessary risks in any area of your life.
Year of the Sheep	A good year financially. Be flexible with your plans.
Year of the Monkey	Working hard at your relationships will pay off.
Year of the Rooster	A busy and enjoyable year, with lots to celebrate.
Year of the Dog	Don't let worries get you down. Be patient.
Year of the Pig	Consolidate the progress you've made but watch your finances.

THE FUTURE FOR THE OX

Here is a brief summary of what the Ox can expect in the following animal years:

Year of the Rat	An excellent year for your finances and for making new investments.
Year of the Ox	New relationships abound, both for business and pleasure.
Year of the Tiger	Patience will help you to get the results you want.
Year of the Rabbit	Use wisdom and caution in all financial matters.
Year of the Dragon	Hard work brings rewards, and so does clever networking.
Year of the Snake	Adopt a flexible attitude for the greatest success this year.
Year of the Horse	Avoid over-committing yourself in any area of your life.
Year of the Sheep	Relationships take precedence over progress in your career.
Year of the Monkey	Life is going well. A cherished dream will come true.
Year of the Rooster	A very enjoyable, successful and happy year.
Year of the Dog	Problems with others aren't as serious as they seem.
Year of the Pig	Establish good contacts with lots of different people.

THE FUTURE FOR THE TIGER

Here is a brief summary of what the Tiger can expect in the following animal years:

Year of the Rat	An uneventful year. Avoid rash and heedless actions.
Year of the Ox	Problems that arise will easily be resolved if you stay calm.
Year of the Tiger	A happy and prosperous year. Avoid being complacent.
Year of the Rabbit	Success in your career and relationships.
Year of the Dragon	Don't cling on to the past when it would be much wiser to let it go.
Year of the Snake	Don't get involved in other people's problems.
Year of the Horse	A fabulous year, both at home and in the wider world.
Year of the Sheep	Happiness comes from being grateful for everything that you have.
Year of the Monkey	Learn to compromise to avoid personality clashes.
Year of the Rooster	Any problems that arise are easily sorted out. Don't panic.
Year of the Dog	Focus on your goals and ambitions, and watch them succeed.
Year of the Pig	Be careful about whom you trust, especially financially.

THE FUTURE FOR THE RABBIT

Here is a brief summary of what the Rabbit can expect in the following animal years:

Year of the Rat	A good year for making plans and achieving them.
Year of the Ox	Frustrations abound because it's hard to make progress.
Year of the Tiger	Avoid clashes and misunderstandings with others.
Year of the Rabbit	A wonderful year on all fronts, with much happiness.
Year of the Dragon	Finances aren't great but your relationships flourish.
Year of the Snake	Prepare for many changes, not all of which will come easily.
Year of the Horse	Cultivate influential people who'll be very useful to you.
Year of the Sheep	Success and happiness in both finances and relationships.
Year of the Monkey	Most relationships flourish but one person can't be trusted.
Year of the Rooster	Teamwork is the way forward. Your finances are lackluster.
Year of the Dog	Despite obstacles, it's a happy year with plenty to enjoy.
Year of the Pig	A good year if you can avoid being naïve or too trusting.

THE FUTURE FOR THE DRAGON

Here is a brief summary of what the Dragon can expect in the following animal years:

Year of the Rat	A busy but enjoyable year. Romance is on the cards.
Year of the Ox	Other people encounter problems but you remain unscathed.
Year of the Tiger	You're caught between warring parties. Keep calm.
Year of the Rabbit	Plenty of progress and happiness. Family life is enjoyable.
Year of the Dragon	Great for your career, leading to recognition and success.
Year of the Snake	Your career flourishes but don't ignore your relationships.
Year of the Horse	A lively year, with many changes and unexpected events.
Year of the Sheep	Relationships bring you the greatest contentment.
Year of the Monkey	Keep others sweet by creating harmony.
Year of the Rooster	A year of great progress and financial prosperity.
Year of the Dog	Difficulties lead to tensions and personality clashes.
Year of the Pig	Life is improving on all levels. Recent problems will melt away.

THE FUTURE FOR THE SNAKE

Here is a brief summary of what the Snake can expect in the following animal years:

Year of the Rat	A busy year with many opportunities for growth.
Year of the Ox	There are obstacles but you also enjoy plenty of success.
Year of the Tiger	A tricky year with disputes in your partnerships.
Year of the Rabbit	The potential for great prosperity but also for overspending.
Year of the Dragon	Life becomes much easier as the year progresses.
Year of the Snake	Stick with the status quo and be patient.
Year of the Horse	A fantastic year when some of your dreams come true.
Year of the Sheep	You meet some influential and helpful people.
Year of the Monkey	Avoid getting involved in other people's disputes.
Year of the Rooster	A wonderful year. All your hard work is now starting to pay off.
Year of the Dog	Be adventurous, enterprising, and optimistic.
Year of the Pig	Avoid rushing into decisions without thinking them through.

THE FUTURE FOR THE HORSE

Here is a brief summary of what the Horse can expect in the following animal years:

Year of the Rat	Be careful and cautious in all financial matters.
Year of the Ox	Hard work pays off. Stay in control of your life.
Year of the Tiger	A lively and enjoyable year. Your spending is high.
Year of the Rabbit	A wonderful year. Travel is very enjoyable.
Year of the Dragon	Don't let life's ups and downs get on your nerves.
Year of the Snake	Progress is sporadic and erratic. Be patient.
Year of the Horse	Success falls into your lap as if by magic.
Year of the Sheep	A change of location is likely. Your life runs smoothly.
Year of the Monkey	Unexpected gains and enjoyable surprises.
Year of the Rooster	Problems can be overcome more easily than you think.
Year of the Dog	Enjoy using your brain. Other people will be impressed.
Year of the Pig	Frustrations and delays gradually resolve themselves.

THE FUTURE FOR THE SHEEP

Here is a brief summary of what the Sheep can expect in the following animal years:

Year of the Rat	Life is good financially, emotionally, and in business.
Year of the Ox	Watch out for clashes and disputes. Be prudent financially.
Year of the Tiger	A happy home life and success in your career.
Year of the Rabbit	You're riding high financially and with long-term plans.
Year of the Dragon	A good year but be careful when handling your money.
Year of the Snake	Plenty of progress, despite setbacks. Travel is enjoyable.
Year of the Horse	A long-running problem has a happy and beneficial outcome.
Year of the Sheep	A difficult year after an excellent start.
Year of the Monkey	A great year, especially in your career and plans.
Year of the Rooster	Plenty of fun and enjoyment, but it's expensive.
Year of the Dog	Not a good year for expansion or risks. Play safe.
Year of the Pig	Be wary of others but don't be too suspicious of them.

THE FUTURE FOR THE MONKEY

Here is a brief summary of what the Monkey can expect in the following animal years:

Year of the Rat	A good year with unexpected gains. Family life is happy.
Year of the Ox	Don't over-stretch yourself. Stick with what you know.
Year of the Tiger	You feel vulnerable, cautious and wary of others.
Year of the Rabbit	Be optimistic and enterprising. Seize opportunities.
Year of the Dragon	A fantastic year for learning something new.
Year of the Snake	Your career goes well but relationships are tricky.
Year of the Horse	Avoid being over-ambitious in your career and goals.
Year of the Sheep	Money flows in and out of your life with ease.
Year of the Monkey	Taking the initiative pays off in many ways.
Year of the Rooster	Your plans are successful but don't over-commit yourself.
Year of the Dog	Learn from your experiences and all will be well.
Year of the Pig	Be careful about whom you trust. Not everyone is honest.

THE FUTURE FOR THE ROOSTER

Here is a brief summary of what the Rooster can expect in the following animal years:

Year of the Rat	A testing year, both financially and emotionally.
Year of the Ox	People are supportive and encouraging. Travel is good fun.
Year of the Tiger	Good career moves lead to an increase in your finances.
Year of the Rabbit	Teamwork is productive. Play safe with your money.
Year of the Dragon	A year of rewarding success and enjoyable prosperity.
Year of the Snake	You make great progress. Show financial prudence.
Year of the Horse	You meet many obstacles but you'll overcome them.
Year of the Sheep	A happy, enjoyable, and emotionally satisfying year.
Year of the Monkey	Be cautious and don't spread yourself too thinly.
Year of the Rooster	Problems melt away and you gain the support of influential people.
Year of the Dog	An enjoyable year, with plenty of travel and progress.
Year of the Pig	An unpredictable year. Be wary of taking risks.

THE FUTURE FOR THE DOG

Here is a brief summary of what the Dog can expect in the following animal years:

Year of the Rat	A great year in career, health and financial matters.
Year of the Ox	You're unsure of your ground. Don't make hasty decisions.
Year of the Tiger	Everything goes well. Relationships are enjoyable.
Year of the Rabbit	Concentrate on your goals and long-term dreams.
Year of the Dragon	You face hard work and struggle to make progress.
Year of the Snake	You taste success on every level. Relax and enjoy it.
Year of the Horse	A marvelous year for all areas of your life.
Year of the Sheep	Be patient, especially in your relationships.
Year of the Monkey	A busy year, with travel or a possible house move.
Year of the Rooster	Temporary setbacks make life difficult.
Year of the Dog	A good year for your career and for learning new skills.
Year of the Pig	Friends are supportive, loyal, and enjoyable company.

THE FUTURE FOR THE PIG

Here is a brief summary of what the Pig can expect in the following animal years:

Year of the Rat   An unsettled year but you'll win through in the end.

Year of the Ox   Capitalize on your many talents and abilities.

Year of the Tiger   A tricky year. Be cautious and prudent with
                           your money.

Year of the Rabbit   You enjoy prosperity and a happy home life.

Year of the Dragon   A great year for working as part of a team.

Year of the Snake   Close partners need to be handled with care.

Year of the Horse   A beneficial year but be sensible with your money.

Year of the Sheep   Make plans for the future. Your career blossoms.

Year of the Monkey   Problems are easily solved with the help of others.

Year of the Rooster   Your home life is happy but your career is tricky.

Year of the Dog   Past problems need to be dealt with once and for all.

Year of the Pig   A good year. New friends brighten up your life.

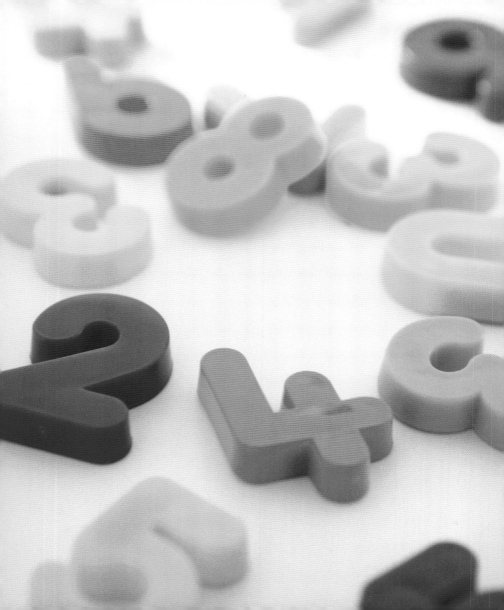

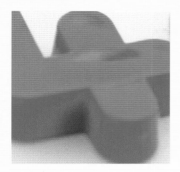

PART FOUR

Numerology

HOW NUMEROLOGY WORKS

Numbers are magical. According to Pythagoras, the 6th-century BCE Greek mathematician who developed what has become the modern system of numerology, they are the building blocks of the universe because he believed that numbers rule nature. To a numerologist, everything in the world is ruled by a number that describes its nature and essence.

Analyzing the numerological value of your name and your date of birth gives you valuable information about your character. As you will discover, you can divide your name into three categories to understand different facets of your character. You can even change your name if you don't like its numerological meaning. Your date of birth, however, is immutable and therefore describes the essential you. No wonder it is called the destiny number.

Pythagoras is considered to be the father of modern numerology.

However, the uses of numerology don't stop at your name and date of birth. You can use it to analyze any names in your life, such as your partner's, or children's.

THE NUMBERS OF NUMEROLOGY

Eleven numbers are used in numerology—the numbers from one to nine, plus 11 and 22. These last two are called master numbers, because they aren't reduced any further. Any other number consisting of two or more digits is always added together until one of the eleven numbers is reached. For instance, 463 is treated like this:

$4 + 6 + 3 = 13, 1 + 3 = 4$.

You calculate the value of a name or word using a system in which each letter is assigned a particular number from one to nine. When you've added up each number, you add the numbers of the total together and continue to reduce it until you reach one of the numerology numbers.

THE NUMEROLOGY SYSTEM

Although some numerology books contain more complicated systems, this is the easiest one to use. You can use it to analyze peoples' names as well as the names of houses, companies, and anything else that interests you.

1	2	3	4	5	6	7	8	9
A	B	C	D	E	F	G	H	I
J	K	L	M	N	O	P	Q	R
S	T	U	V	W	X	Y	Z	

CALCULATING THE NUMBERS

Let's say that you want to analyze your name. When doing this, you should use the name by which you are normally known. For instance, if your real name is Susanna Wendy Maples but you always call yourself Wendy Maples, this is the name you should analyze.

VOWELS OR CONSONANTS?

The first step is to write out your name and assign a number to each letter using the chart on the previous page. Write the numbers for the vowels above the name and the numbers for the consonants below the name. If there is a Y in the name you must decide how to treat it. Some numerologists always consider it to be a vowel. Others say it's a vowel if it's pronounced but a consonant if it's silent.

It's a good idea to keep all your numerological calculations in a special notebook so you've got them all in one place.

WORKING OUT THE NUMBERS

Try analyzing your own name using the example below, writing the numbers for the vowels above the name and the numbers for consonants below.

5				7		1			5	
W	E	N	D	Y	M	A	P	L	E	S
5		5	4		4		7	3		1

THE HEART NUMBER

Add up the number of vowels in Wendy's name: **5 + 7 + 1+ 5 = 18; 1 + 8 = 9**. The number **9** is Wendy's heart number, meaning it describes her deepest wishes and desires.

THE EXPRESSION NUMBER

Add up the number of consonants in Wendy's name: **5 + 5 + 4 + 4 + 7 + 3 + 1 = 29; 2 + 9 = 11**. The number **11** is Wendy's expression number, describing the image she presents to the world. Eleven is a master number and therefore can't be reduced any further.

THE PERSONALITY NUMBER

To find this number you add together the heart and expression numbers. For Wendy, this is: **9** (heart number) **+ 11** (expression number) **= 20; 2 + 0 = 2**.

THE DESTINY NUMBER

Finally, you calculate the destiny number by adding together the numbers in a person's date of birth. Wendy was born on December 11, 1988. You translate each month into its numerical equivalent, with January being **1** and December being **12**. For Wendy, this works out as: **1 + 1 + 1+ 2 + 1 + 9 + 8 +8 = 31; 3 + 1 = 4**. Therefore, Wendy's destiny number is **4**.

ONE

This very powerful number is linked to beginnings. It is the first masculine number and relates to the Sun and the astrological sign of Leo.

PERSONALITY NUMBER

Someone with this powerful personality number can't bear to be restricted and absolutely has to do her own thing. She will soon complain or rebel if she feels she's being held back in some way or hampered by dreary routine. She is creative and inspired, and she needs to express her talents in whichever way feels right to her.

HEART NUMBER

This person's deepest wish is to be independent and original. She wants to be a free spirit and may even avoid committed relationships in order to give herself the freedom she craves. When she is in a relationship she tends to hide the more emotional side of her nature, leading others to suspect that she might not care as much as she actually does.

EXPRESSION NUMBER

This is someone who appears to be in control of her life. She gives the impression of being confident, cheerful, outgoing, and a natural leader, regardless of how she really feels. Others may admire her for apparently having her entire life sorted out. Sometimes she can come across as too self-assured and even slightly aggressive, although this may simply be bravado. Nevertheless, she is a popular member of her social circle.

DESTINY NUMBER

This is someone who has to go her own way: she wants to be a leader, not a follower. She is a pioneer and an innovator, regardless of what other people might think

One is a very creative number, thanks to its association with Leo.

about her chosen path through life. She is single-minded, ambitious, and determined, but can therefore be obstinate. Although she is kind-hearted and warm, she can find it hard to be demonstrative and affectionate.

TWO

A dual number, two rules all opposites and is connected with partnership. It relates to the Moon and the astrological sign of Cancer.

PERSONALITY NUMBER

This person is well-balanced, diplomatic, and good at sorting out other people's problems, although handling her own difficulties can be more of a challenge. She is good at negotiation and mediation, whether in business or in her private life. She has sensitive emotions, is kind and considerate, and very protective of the people she loves. Sometimes she can hold on to belongings, people, or situations long after she should have let them go.

HEART NUMBER

This person may seem to be self-assured and independent (according to her expression number), but underneath she's sensitive, vulnerable, and needy. She is at her best in a close relationship, when she can open up emotionally and take comfort in being part of a team. She enjoys taking care of loved ones and giving them her support and love. Emotional security is very important to her and she works hard to maintain it.

EXPRESSION NUMBER

This person has such a strong drive for perfection that she can be very critical of loved ones, being quick to point out their faults. She is also very tough on herself if she thinks she's failed to live up to her own high standards. It is important for her to be part of a team and to be regarded as a team player, despite her tendency to tell others

what they should be doing. She does her utmost to support the people around her.

DESTINY NUMBER

Someone with this destiny number needs to be in a relationship or to be part of a team: she's unhappy by herself. As a result of her desire to have other people in her life she may often be too

Two is the first feminine number. It's the number of harmonious relationships.

quick to put her own needs second and to let others have their way. Inevitably, this can lead to resentment whenever she feels that she's being taken for granted or that her sacrifices haven't been acknowledged.

THREE

This is the number of all kinds of growth, whether physical or mental. It relates to Jupiter and the astrological sign of Sagittarius.

PERSONALITY NUMBER

Ever positive and optimistic, this person can't help looking on the bright side. As a result, she seems to attract luck and may even lead a charmed life. As a result of her bubbly, sunny, and lively personality, she is very popular and probably has many friends. In her career, she excels at any job that allows her to communicate with others, especially if it offers plenty of variety and scope as well.

HEART NUMBER

Someone with this heart number is warm-hearted, gregarious, and positive. She enjoys being with friends and family, and likes to encourage them. She has an optimistic view of life which she readily shares with others, making her appear to be confident and well-balanced. However,

deep down she is worried about being left alone and ending up lonely. She yearns to be accepted by the people for whom she cares, particularly friends, family, or a partner.

EXPRESSION NUMBER

This person loves being the center of attention, and other people enjoy her company—she's so entertaining and amusing. Her style can be quite flamboyant and dramatic. She may even be attracted to the acting profession. Sometimes, she can come across as rather arrogant and full of herself, but this is bravado that conceals a much more sensitive and reticent side to her character.

DESTINY NUMBER

This person is versatile, lively, and good-humored. She needs to keep moving ahead in her life, with plenty to look forward to and many challenges at which she can aim. She isn't happy when life becomes tedious or predictable, and needs constant change. Her relationships are successful because she's such good fun to be around and people are naturally drawn to her, although she may not be known for her fidelity. She enjoys travel and ideally her job should reflect this.

Three likes to be in contact with many different people.

FOUR

This is the number of stability and practicality. It relates to Saturn and the astrological sign of Capricorn.

PERSONALITY NUMBER

This is someone who is organized, efficient, and who likes to follow a particular routine. He needs his life to run smoothly and will feel very unsettled whenever he hits a crisis. Hard-working and reliable, he can be a little too strict with himself sometimes. Relationships may suffer because of his reluctance to unbend, have fun, or leave his work behind at the office. Nevertheless, he is popular because he's so trustworthy: you know where you are with him.

HEART NUMBER

This person likes to be thought of as dependable and trustworthy, and to know that people rely on him. He prefers to keep out of the limelight and work behind the scenes, and gets uncomfortable when too much attention is focused on him. Shy and sensitive, he needs a happy, secure home life where he can relax. He is a good homemaker and his family will always come first for him. He likes to feel that he can provide for his family.

EXPRESSION NUMBER

Conservative and traditional, this person can come across as rather staid and hidebound. He may even seem wedded to routine and to doing things in a particular order. He is suspicious of people who behave in a very different way because he isn't sure how to handle them or what they're going to do next. His need to do the right thing and to appear reliable can mean he is sometimes taken for granted by more flighty people.

DESTINY NUMBER

Someone born with this destiny number is solidly rooted in reality. He's got his feet on the ground and prides himself on his practical approach to life. Ambition is important to him and he will pursue a goal with determination until he finally achieves it, even if this causes problems in other

Four needs the reassurance and structure that a daily routine can provide.

areas of his life. He likes to stick with what he knows so can be resistant to change, and as a result may sometimes get bogged down in ruts.

FIVE

This is a creative number that is also linked with travel. It relates to Mercury and the astrological signs of Gemini and Virgo.

PERSONALITY NUMBER

This person can be so busy keeping one eye on the future that she forgets to concentrate on what's happening to her in the present. She needs plenty of movement and variety to stave off boredom, and travel is a particular love of hers. Sometimes she will subconsciously manufacture a crisis simply in order to liven things up and provide something new to think about. This strong need for variety can make her restless.

Five needs plenty of mental stimulation, with lots of variety.

HEART NUMBER

Someone with this heart number has a deep need to find kindred spirits, especially if they're on the same intellectual wavelength as her. She often has a nagging suspicion that life is passing her by and that she's missing out on all sorts of wonderful experiences. This can make her flit from one partner to another in the search for the perfect relationship. She is interested in ideas and studying fascinating subjects.

EXPRESSION NUMBER

Lively, chatty, and good fun, this person enjoys having her finger on the pulse of life and especially likes being up on all the latest gossip. She comes across as quite a chatterbox but always has something interesting to say because she's well-read and well-informed. She enjoys a busy social life and has plenty of friends. It's difficult for her to stay in one place for long because she's easily bored, so she enjoys taking off on vacations and long-distance travel.

DESTINY NUMBER

This person needs plenty of mental stimulation and variety in her life to function at her best. Frequent changes of scene are essential to stop her becoming bored and, eventually, depressed. However, she needs to guard against darting from one job or relationship to the next in an endless quest for something new. She's quick-witted and charming, and good fun to be around.

SIX

This is the number of love, not only in relationships but also love of the home. It relates to Venus and the astrological signs of Taurus and Libra.

PERSONALITY NUMBER

This person likes to be successful, both at home and at work. He may be drawn to self-employment, especially in a creative or artistic profession. However, he has strict standards which he expects himself, and everyone else, to fulfill, and is very critical when this doesn't happen. He prides himself on being of service to others. His home and family are very important to him and he does his best to show how much he loves them.

HEART NUMBER

Love is essential to this person's happiness. He needs to know that all his relationships are successful and affectionate, but he places particular importance on his family ties because these are so important to him. He works hard to make his home life as happy, comfortable, and relaxed as possible, and is bitterly disappointed if other people don't reciprocate. Sometimes he may even choose to work from home in order to stay near his family.

EXPRESSION NUMBER

It's important for this person to give a good impression and to come across as stable, efficient, and capable. He's particularly concerned about having a good reputation at work. However, it certainly isn't a question of all work and no play because he likes to enjoy himself whenever he gets the chance and also has a penchant for the good things in life. This can even lead to hedonism and extravagance.

*Relationships are
an integral part
of life for someone
with the
number six.*

DESTINY NUMBER

Home and family are everything to this person, who thrives on a happy domestic life and will suffer if he encounters domestic problems. He's always happiest in familiar surroundings and when he's with people he knows well. He may even be so concerned about keeping loved ones happy and contented that he puts their needs before his own. He has a small social circle that consists of family and carefully chosen friends.

SEVEN

Seven is a mystical and magical number, with strong connections to spirituality. It relates to Neptune and the astrological sign of Pisces.

PERSONALITY NUMBER

Creative and musical, this person is sensitive to the atmosphere around her. She can have memorable dreams that allow her to gain greater insight into her personality and the situations in which she finds herself. She has a slightly mystical view of life and may also be searching for spiritual truths. It suits her to have time to herself, when she can retreat from the world. In relationships she can come across as slightly remote and detached.

HEART NUMBER

Someone with this heart number is sensitive and tuned into an inner, mystical and spiritual world which others don't necessarily understand. As a result, she can sometimes be considered strange. She has a tendency to retreat into this world whenever life gets tough or uncomfortable. As a result, it can be difficult for partners to get really close to her because she always seems to be holding something back, even if she isn't aware of this herself.

EXPRESSION NUMBER

Slightly aloof and reserved, this is someone who isn't easy to know at first. This means she can be misunderstood and wrongly considered to be rude. Her shyness and reticence stop her being as forthcoming as she might like, although she's much more affectionate with people she knows well and with whom she can relax. She's wise, charming, and intelligent, with an interest in all things mystical and spiritual.

DESTINY NUMBER

This person has a strong psychic streak and a powerful intuition, both of which guide her through life. She's introverted and needs plenty of time on her own. She may be interested in meditation or some other form of contemplation. She's blessed with a good imagination but this can sometimes prompt her to worry about things that don't really matter and which might eventually affect her health.

Someone with the number seven is strongly intuitive and may have powerful dreams.

EIGHT

Eight is linked with the material world but it also has spiritual connections. It relates to Saturn and the astrological sign of Capricorn.

PERSONALITY NUMBER

Businesslike and ambitious, this is someone who knows what he wants from life and will do everything he can to get it. He'll work round the clock if necessary in order to reach his goals. As a result, he can become very successful in life, although sometimes at the cost of his relationships which have to come second. He is an excellent organizer and administrator but can be critical of other people's failings.

HEART NUMBER

Eager to be successful, this person will feel that he's let himself down if he doesn't achieve his ambitions. He needs to be seen to succeed, so is likely to be drawn to professions that put him in the public eye. He certainly isn't happy when working quietly in the background for other people. Material success is also important to him and he likes all the trappings that go with it. He's highly organized and finds it difficult to relax.

EXPRESSION NUMBER

Hard-working and efficient, this person can give the impression of being rather bossy. In fact, he's kind-hearted beneath what can be quite a brusque and superior exterior. He would probably be appalled if he knew how others saw him. What can seem like smug and self-satisfied behavior to others is simply him trying to be businesslike and professional. His organizing skills are second to none.

DESTINY NUMBER

This person is geared for success in everything he does. This is partly because he needs material and financial security, but also because he wants to achieve his ambitions and will pursue them until he's successful. He works hard and expects the same determined attitude

Eight is the classic number for someone with a good business brain.

from partners, employees, and colleagues. His relationships may suffer, with partners suspecting that his career will always come first.

NINE

This is a very spiritual number but it is also connected with energy and drive. It relates to Mars and the astrological signs of Aries and Scorpio.

PERSONALITY NUMBER

Patience may be in short supply for this person, who likes things to happen quickly and according to her own timetable. She soon gets annoyed if she has to wait for others to catch up with her fast pace. Despite this, she has a strongly humanitarian streak and is especially supportive if someone is having a crisis. She's loyal and considerate with partners, although it can take her a while to settle down with a lifelong partner.

HEART NUMBER

Endlessly curious about the world, this person is always keen to discover what's going on around her. She's inquisitive and can be nosy, not appreciating when it's inappropriate to pry into other people's affairs. As a result, there can sometimes be tension with friends and partners. She needs lots of variety in her life, which can make her changeable, quixotic, and rather restless at times.

EXPRESSION NUMBER

Lively and interesting, this person is highly dynamic. She's good company and exudes an attraction that wins her many fans. Perhaps because of this, she may not be very faithful to partners. Even if she only flirts with other people, she needs a partner who understands her desire for emotional freedom and independence. She isn't noted for her time-keeping or her tact, and has a tendency to say exactly what she thinks.

DESTINY NUMBER

This person is charitable, compassionate, and kind, with a strong visionary streak. Unhappy childhood experiences may have prompted her to adopt an idealistic view of how life should be. She has high ideals and works hard to put them into practice. It's

Someone with the number nine is kind but can have a short fuse.

very important for her to achieve her ambitions, and she can grow impatient with herself if she fails to get the results she wants quickly enough.

ELEVEN

The first of the two master numbers, 11 is connected to strength and psychic gifts. It relates to Uranus and the astrological sign of Aquarius.

PERSONALITY NUMBER

This person is a born communicator, full of charisma and charm, who could easily be attracted to a career in the media as a journalist or an actor. Alternatively, he might be an inspirational teacher who excels at getting his message across to his pupils. Relationships, however, can be problematic because of his desire to forge a name for himself and his need to be successful in his career.

HEART NUMBER

Here is someone who has a mission in life and who is often gripped by idealistic zeal and the need to make the world a better place. Once he's found his purpose in life he'll stick to it with dogged determination, regardless of what other people might think or say. He may even take risks in order to fulfill his goals. He's able to draw on his self-confidence and crusading spirit, which keep him going during difficult times.

EXPRESSION NUMBER

This person is idealistic and inspired, and often has strong spiritual beliefs. He likes to know that others support him in what he does and is very disappointed when they don't. He has a strong creative streak which he needs to express in whichever ways come most naturally to him. Such creativity can lead to a successful career but sometimes he can waste a lot of energy by chasing rainbows and impossible dreams.

DESTINY NUMBER

There's no doubting this person's leadership capacity and his determination to achieve whatever he sets out to do. He has an iron will and is able to push himself to extraordinary lengths whenever he feels it's necessary. He has high ideals, too, so feels he cannot abandon his goals. However, his relationships suffer from such strong ambitions because he may not be able to devote much time or energy to them.

Eleven is a very powerful number, with the potential to inspire others.

TWENTY-TWO

The second of the two master numbers, 22 is linked with perfection. It relates to Neptune and the astrological sign of Pisces.

PERSONALITY NUMBER

Tremendously capable and talented, this person has the ability to stand out from the crowd. However, she may not make the most of her own talents because they come so easily to her and she has a tendency to take them for granted. She is very attractive, with a magnetic personality, and has a host of fans. This can spark off jealousy in her partners if they feel insecure about the place they hold in her heart.

HEART NUMBER

Here is someone with a deep need to make a difference in the world and to improve it in some way. She's particularly drawn to humanitarian causes but can find it hard to follow them whenever the going gets tough. It may be easier for her to imagine doing good than to do it in reality. Even so, she

has enormous potential and is capable of achieving a great deal, provided that she persists whenever she's tempted to give up.

EXPRESSION NUMBER

This person is very wise, and therefore is often consulted by friends and family who need her help. At times, she's capable of extraordinary compassion and empathy, which wins her many friends and makes her greatly loved. She's good at assessing the people around her, despite an idealistic streak. She's likely to make a success of her life and to be financially rewarded for it, although she may feel that other people are more deserving causes.

DESTINY NUMBER

This person is blessed with considerable gifts and talents, which she normally puts

to very good use. In fact, she seems to be able to turn her hand to almost anything, which can lead to a sense of complacency if she isn't careful. She can also be tempted to take the easy way out of challenges and other difficult situations. Her relationships can suffer because of her occasional inability to assess peoples' personalities properly.

Twenty-two is a very humanitarian number, with a strong urge to help other people.

CALCULATING YOUR YEAR NUMBERS

As well as discovering your destiny number by adding up the numbers in your date of birth, you can also calculate the numerological theme of a particular year.

This is useful at any time of year but is especially informative at the start of the year, when you want to gain some insight into what opportunities the coming 12 months will bring you.

ADDING UP THE YEAR

This is a very simple technique. All you do is to add the day and month of your birth to the year in question. You then look up the number in question in the relevant section of this chapter to determine the theme of that year. For instance, if you want to discover the theme of 2010 for you, all you do is to add the numbers of the year to those of the date and month of your birth. So, if you were born on February 13 (which is the second month of the year), the calculation would look like this:

1 + 3 + 2 + 2 + 0 + 1 + 0 = 9.

This means that 2010 would be a year in which the main theme for you related to the number nine, so it would be about spirituality and energy.

LOOKING BACK

You can also use this technique to look back over special years in your life, which will give you some valuable insight into the way their numbers have affected you. For instance, you might find that years related to the number six, which is connected to love, have always been years in which you met someone special or have had a very happy time with friends and family. Although you might imagine that the years always run in a consecutive cycle of one to nine, in fact they don't because occasionally there will be an 11 or 22 year. These may be landmark years, because they are ruled by master numbers.

Look back at important years in your life to see which numbers they are ruled by.

CHANGING YOUR NAME

Most of us like the names we're given at birth, but sometimes we want to find a name that suits us better. Maybe you dislike the name you were given and wish you could find something more suitable. How do you choose it?

Numerology is one way in which to do this, because you can calculate the numerological meaning of your new name to discover whether it suits you. Ideally, your destiny number (the number of your date of birth) should be harmonious with your personality number (the number of the name by which you're known), and both should either be odd or even numbers.

FINDING A PSEUDONYM

Perhaps you're perfectly happy with your real name but you'd like to find a pseudonym, whether it's for use in internet chat rooms or for professional reasons. Again, you can use numerology to find the perfect name. Think of some names that appeal to you and then calculate their numerological value to discover whether they're suitable. For instance, if you're looking for a new partner, you might choose an internet name that adds up to two, which is the number for relationships.

CHOOSING A BUSINESS NAME

Numerology is particularly useful when it comes to choosing a business name. If you want your business to be successful and make money, it makes sense to choose a name whose numerological value reflects these aims. Alternatively, maybe you want your business name's number to describe the nature of the business. So, if you wanted to open a shop that sells crystals, tarot cards, and similar merchandise, you could choose a number that adds up to nine (spirituality) or 11 (psychic talents). But if you're starting a building firm, you would be wise to choose a name that adds up to four, which is the number of stability and practicality.

Numerology can help you choose a pseudonym for use in internet chat rooms.

HOUSE NAMES AND NUMBERS

Numerology can give you a lot of useful information about the energy of the name or number of your house. Is it a house whose energy you like and which is integrated with yours, or have you always wondered why you felt uncomfortable there or why various projects that you wanted to get off the ground failed to materialize? Numerology will help to give you the answers!

CALCULATING YOUR HOUSE'S NAME OR NUMBER

If you live in a house with a number, you follow exactly the same process that you used for calculating your destiny number (see pages 102–103). If the house number is a single number, or is either 11 or 22, you don't have to reduce it any further. However, if you live in a house with a larger number, such as 1036, you must add the numbers together until you reach one of the numerology numbers:

$1 + 0 + 3 + 6 = 10; 1 + 0 = 1.$

If you live in a house with a name, you follow exactly the same processes that you used for calculating your personality, heart and expression numbers (see pages 102–103). If you have a strong feel for numerology you may wish to pay attention to the heart and expression numbers of your house name. Alternatively, you may prefer to concentrate on its personality number instead.

CHANGING YOUR HOUSE'S NAME

If you don't like the numerological meaning of your house's number, you may not be able to change it. However, there's no reason why you can't give it a suitable name and use that instead. If your house already has a name and either you don't like it or you don't like its numerological meaning, once again you can change it. Choose a name with an appropriate numerological meaning and then follow the laws that apply when you want to change a house name: these will vary from one country to the next so be sure to investigate further before making the change.

Use numerology to choose a suitable name for your house.

SAMPLE NUMEROLOGICAL READING

There are many ways to give numerological readings, depending on what the person is looking for. Someone might simply want to gain a greater understanding of the numbers of her name and birth date, while another person may want to use numerology to help his business.

Johnnie Brown wanted to choose the right name for his new business, which was a shop selling bicycles. His main aim with the shop was to make money and he wanted to be so successful that he could start a chain of shops. The first step was to calculate his own numbers, which would provide a good insight into his personality and business aptitude.

This gives him a personality number of three, with a heart number of eight and an expression number of four. His eight heart number is the clue to his financial and business ambitions.

THE FIRST STEP

We start by analyzing the name of the person who will own the business, to get a good idea of what he's like and what he wants.

6	9 5	6	= 26 = 2 + 6 = **8** (heart)	
J O H N N I E	B R O W N			
1 8 5 5	2 9 5 5	= 40 = 4 + 0 = **4** (expression)		

8 (heart) + **4** (expression) = **12** = 1 + 2 = **3** (personality)

The next step was to calculate his destiny number from his birth date of November 1, 1967. This added up to eight, which once again revealed his ambitious streak.

Johnnie said he couldn't decide whether to call his new business Brown's Bikes or Brown's Bicycles.

Brown's Bikes had a personality number of two, with a heart number of 11 and an expression number of nine. It wasn't a great combination for a business that was intended to make money.

Brown's Bicycles, however, had a personality number of eight, with a heart number of 11 and an expression number of six. This personality number was a much better reflection of Johnnie's ambitions and also of his own heart number.

THE FIRST OPTION

This is the breakdown of the first name that Johnnie considered. It doesn't reflect his business ambitions.

	6						9		5	
B	R	O	W	N	S	B	I	K	E	S
2	9		5	5	1	2		2		1

THE SECOND OPTION

This is the breakdown of the second name. The eight personality number matches Johnnie's destiny and heart numbers.

	6						9					5	
B	R	O	W	N	S	B	I	C	Y	C	L	E	S
2	9		5	5	1	2		3	7	3	3		1

PART FIVE

The Tarot

HOW THE TAROT WORKS

The 78 cards that comprise the tarot are powerful predictive tools, helping you to analyze situations and gain insight into what the future holds for you.

Many different kinds of tarot cards are available, ranging from traditional designs to specialized decks that focus on a particular theme.

When you first examine a deck of tarot cards, the images may seem unfamiliar or even alarming to you. Cards such as Death and the Hanged Man have helped to contribute to the tarot's reputation for being sinister, but in fact the cards' meanings aren't as grim as they first appear and they shouldn't be taken literally. When the tarot first appeared in medieval Europe, it contained images from spiritual and religious beliefs that were out of favor at the time. The symbols and images on the cards were a secret, coded language that enabled the adherents of forbidden practices such as astrology to make contact with one another without the authorities being any the wiser. Many decks are still rich in symbolism that will help to deepen your readings.

FINDING THE RIGHT DECK FOR YOU

One of the most important aspects of working with the tarot is to find the right deck for you. Do you want one in which every card is illustrated with its meaning? Are you happiest with a traditional or a contemporary design? Ideally, you should browse through several decks before making up your mind, choosing the one that appeals to you the most and which feels right.

ARCANA—MAJOR AND MINOR

The tarot consists of two sections: the 22 cards of the Major Arcana and the 56 cards of the Minor Arcana. The Major Arcana refers to our journey through life, including many of the important events that we can expect to meet along the way. The Minor Arcana, which is divided into four suits, describes the more everyday incidents we can expect to encounter. As a result,

Tarot has been popular for several centuries.
The earliest known cards were painted in
the early 15th century in Italy.

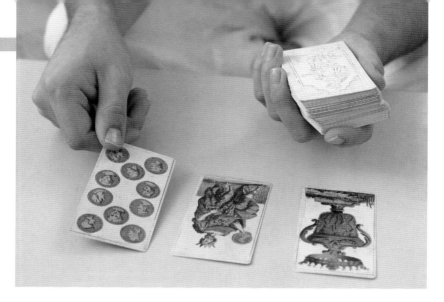

Simple layouts of three cards can be remarkably informative.

readings that contain an above-average number of Major Arcana cards refer to circumstances that are beyond our control, whereas readings with an above-average number of Minor Arcana cards refer to situations that we can control and alter if we wish to do so.

GIVING A READING

You read the tarot by shuffling the cards while thinking of the question you want to ask, and then you deal them out into a particular pattern, known as a spread. You

then interpret each card according to its position in the spread. For instance, if the Ace of Cups falls in the position that describes your relationships, it suggests that you will be embarking on a new partnership.

IS A READING ALWAYS CORRECT?

A common misunderstanding about the tarot is that the predictions it makes will automatically happen, which is one of the reasons why cards such as the Hanged Man have the power to shock. In fact, the tarot's predictions don't always come true, for a number of reasons. One factor might be that you've misinterpreted a card, perhaps because you imagine it's talking about one thing when actually it refers to something else. Another possibility is that the situation surrounding the reading changes and therefore alters the outcome. This is especially likely if the cards give you a warning about a difficult situation and you then take avoiding action.

CHOOSE THE TIME OF THE READING CAREFULLY

The tarot acts like a mirror, reflecting situations back to us so we can see them clearly. This means that it also has a tendency to reflect our moods, which is why it isn't a good idea to have a tarot reading when you're feeling agitated. The tarot will simply reflect your situation straight back to you. Wait until you're feeling calmer before consulting the cards. You should also avoid consulting the tarot too often, especially concerning the same questions. If you keep asking the tarot the same question it will eventually begin to talk nonsense to you. You must treat tarot with respect if you want it to work properly and give you good readings.

The Celtic Cross is an excellent all-around spread that provides lots of detail.

THE MAJOR AND MINOR ARCANA

*As mentioned earlier there are 22 cards in the Major Arcana and
56 cards in the Minor Arcana. The cards of the Minor Arcana are not
always illustrated.*

At first, the thought of learning the
meanings of all 78 tarot cards can be
daunting, which is why some people prefer
to concentrate on the 22 cards of the Major
Arcana. Although these are undoubtedly
powerful cards, using them without the 56
cards of the Minor Arcana can give slightly
unbalanced readings that lack the subtle
details conferred by the Minor Arcana.

THE MAJOR ARCANA

Most tarot decks start with the Fool. This
card is either unnumbered or bears the
figure 0, to show that it is both the
beginning and end of a cycle. Some decks
have slight variations on the names of the
cards in the Major Arcana and there are
also differences in their running order. The
names and sequence of the cards given
here are those most commonly used.

0 THE FOOL

This is the classic card of beginnings. It describes the excitement, enthusiasm, and optimism that usually accompany fresh starts. However, there may be something foolhardy about the new venture, with the possibility that you will rush into it without thinking it through. Alternatively, other people may denigrate your plans even though you are convinced that you are on the right track. The card is warning you to check that your plans are feasible and won't lead you into dangerous territory, before proceeding with them.

I THE MAGICIAN

As his name suggests, the Magician is a powerful figure. The card may describe an influential person who enters your life, in which case it is warning you to be wary because there may be some trickery or deceit. Alternatively, the card describes you, and is saying that you have more power and ability than you realize. You must find ways of releasing and expressing these talents, and you are already equipped with the means with which to do this.

II THE HIGH PRIESTESS

This is the card of intuition, instincts, and psychic ability. It's telling you to trust your gut feelings and also to pay attention to your dreams, as these will have important messages for you. Be open to the messages that are being sent to you. The High Priestess can also signify a period in which you will discover a great deal about life, either through formal study or simply by learning from experience. Spiritual studies are especially likely when this card appears.

III THE EMPRESS

The Empress represents fertility, abundance, and creativity in all their forms. This card often crops up when you need to spend more time in the open air or surrounded by nature, and sometimes she describes moving to a home in lovely surroundings. She can also describe physical or metaphorical fertility, whether it's the birth of a child, the cultivation of land, or the arrival of a new idea. In all these circumstances the outlook is favorable because the Empress is a very positive card.

IV THE EMPEROR

The Emperor has a very stern quality. He speaks of grim authority, of being prepared to go into battle when necessary, and of the need to maintain control. Very often, this card says that you will soon have authority conferred on you, perhaps through a new job or increased social status. The Emperor is also telling you to stick to your guns if you need to stand up for yourself. Alternatively, the card describes someone you know who has a lot of power and who is reliable. You can trust this person to do the right thing.

V THE HIEROPHANT

When this card appears in a spread, it's telling you to do things in a tried and tested manner. This isn't a time for launching out bravely with unconventional schemes. Instead, you need to play by the rules and do things traditionally. The Hierophant can also describe the need to introduce greater spiritual purpose and meaning into your life. When the card represents someone else, this person is conventional, traditional, and reliable, possibly with a strong faith.

VI THE LOVERS

This card has two meanings. The first, as its name suggests, refers to a loving relationship. This may be a romantic or sexual connection but it's just as likely to be platonic or familial. If the relationship has been going through a difficult phase lately, the Lovers urges you to repair the rift and put it behind you. The second meaning concerns a choice, especially if some form of sacrifice is involved. For instance, you may have to make a choice between having creative fulfillment or earning more money.

VII THE CHARIOT

The Chariot is telling you to use your willpower and determination to cope with a difficult situation, such as a tricky relationship, an uphill struggle, or a character-forming challenge. Brute force and other strong-arm tactics won't work; instead, you must grit your teeth and get on with the task before you. The Chariot doesn't promise instant results but it does reassure you that everything will eventually come right, provided that you behave in a fair manner and don't rush into anything.

VIII STRENGTH

This card encourages you to do the seemingly impossible, assuring you that you'll be successful. You are being presented with a difficult task that will be easier than you think. Approach the challenge with strength of purpose and self-belief, and without being heavy-handed. You must know when to hold back and when to push forward to your advantage. The card refers to many different types of strength, whether physical, moral, or emotional. Sometimes it describes a successful convalescence after an illness.

IX THE HERMIT

The Hermit is encouraging you to shed light on a situation. This might mean enlightening yourself by learning something new, perhaps through formal education. It could refer to a spiritual test that you must undergo in order to gain greater insight into your own character, or it might describe receiving Divine consolation during a difficult experience. Very often this card describes a period of solitude and contemplation. Sometimes the Hermit warns that you've yet to learn all the facts about a particular situation.

X THE WHEEL OF FORTUNE

This is one of the cards describing major change and the end of a cycle. If you're going through a difficult phase, the Wheel of Fortune reminds you that nothing lasts forever and that the situation will soon alter. It can describe external circumstances, such as material difficulties or emotional problems, or inner dilemmas. This card reminds us that life is continually changing, so even happy and prosperous circumstances may give way to troublesome phases.

XI JUSTICE

As its name suggests, this card describes the need to behave in a judicial and fair manner. Sometimes it appears at the time of a court case or some other legal action, when it counsels you to be moderate and to play fair if you wish to be successful. Whatever the situation you find yourself in, Justice warns against going to extremes. Instead, you must find a sense of balance in your life. If a relationship is going through the doldrums you should strive to see the other person's point of view and to find a compromise between you.

XII THE HANGED MAN

The Hanged Man has two meanings. The first is being caught in limbo and having to wait patiently for the next phase in your life to start. This may involve some form of sacrifice or penalty, such as a financial expense, but there is nothing you can do about this. The second meaning is that you need to view a situation from a completely different perspective in order to understand it better. This is no time to cling to your fixed opinions.

XIII DEATH

This is another card describing major change. Although the card is called "Death," it usually speaks of a symbolic death, such as a time of tremendous transformation in your life or a great psychological insight that changes you. The old order is dying and a chapter in your life is coming to an end, but something new will soon arrive to take its place. Although this experience may be difficult at the time, it is necessary for your spiritual and psychological growth, as you'll soon realize.

XIV TEMPERANCE

Temperance urges you to be more moderate and balanced in your life, and not to go to extremes in any way. If you've been working too hard, you need to slow down and cultivate the other areas of your life. If you've been eating or drinking the wrong things, it's time to choose a healthier diet. This card also encourages you to balance and satisfy both your material and spiritual needs, advising you that you can't have one without the other.

XV THE DEVIL

The Devil describes enslavement and the feeling of being caught in something from which you can't escape. This might be a difficult situation from which you feel there is no way out, such as a dead-end job with no better prospects around the corner. Alternatively, the Devil can describe an addiction, whether it is to a relationship, an emotional attitude, or a particular substance, such as alcohol. Although you may feel trapped, in fact there is a solution if you are prepared to look for it.

XVI THE TOWER

The Tower describes a dramatic event that happens very suddenly, like a bolt from the blue. Very often, this involves a fall from grace or a sense of embarrassment. For instance, it might be a very public financial downturn or a failed relationship. Although the crisis described by the Tower appears to have arrived out of nowhere, in fact it has been brewing for a while and is happening for a reason. Difficult though it is at the time, it usually turns out to be a blessing in disguise.

XVII THE STAR

This is the wish card of the Major Arcana, so it often tells you that a cherished wish will soon be granted. If you've been going through a difficult phase or a period of ill health, better times are on the way. It encourages you to be optimistic and to trust that everything will turn out for the best. The Star can also refer to an enterprise or relationship that will give you spiritual nourishment and emotional satisfaction, but warns you not to concentrate on it to the exclusion of all else.

XVIII THE MOON

Be careful, because all is not what it seems when the Moon appears in a spread. A situation may develop in ways you weren't anticipating, especially if some form of deceit or double-dealing is involved. This might be because someone will trick you, or it may be because you aren't seeing the situation in its true light. Perhaps you are afraid to face facts and would prefer to hide behind rosy illusions? The Moon can also describe confusion or muddles that need to be sorted out, or facts that must be clarified before they can be understood.

XIX THE SUN

One of the most positive tarot cards, the Sun describes happiness, joy, and contentment. These might come from a fulfilling relationship, such as a love affair, or the loving connection between parent and child. Sometimes, it foretells the birth of a child or of a satisfying creative project. If you have been going through a difficult experience, the Sun promises that your trials and tribulations will soon come to an end. It can also refer to travel to a hot country.

XX JUDGMENT

This card has several meanings. The first is receiving or giving someone a second chance. It might indicate that you need to give someone the benefit of the doubt if you've fallen out with them lately, or that you shouldn't abandon a challenge at the first hurdle. It can also represent some form of rebirth. Judgment carries a warning against being too judgmental of others, and of laying all the blame at their feet while not recognizing your own failings.

XXI THE WORLD

The World is one of the cards signifying major change, because it marks the end of one cycle and the start of another. It can indicate success and triumph, especially in worldly terms, and it can also suggest that you have many more options available than you realize. As its name suggests, the World is also connected with travel, and can describe an enjoyable or significant journey, or emigration to another country.

THE SUIT OF WANDS

One of four suits in the Minor Arcana, Wands are connected with taking risks, with speculation and enterprise. They also rule travel, imagination, and intuition, as well as career aspirations. They correspond to Clubs in playing cards, and in Western astrology to the three Fire signs of Aries, Leo, and Sagittarius.

ACE
This signifies the exciting birth of a new project or enterprise, especially if it involves speculation, enterprise, or travel.

TWO
Take stock of what you've achieved and what you have yet to accomplish. An opportunity is on the way.

THREE
You are in a good position but you must wait patiently for the results of your efforts so far.

FOUR
Hard work leads to a celebration. Sometimes a successful house move or an enjoyable vacation is indicated.

FIVE
An irritating phase in which your plans are thwarted or you encounter opposition from others.

SIX
An enjoyable time of triumph and achievement. Don't rest on your laurels because more hard work is ahead of you.

SEVEN

You are facing a lot of competition, but you need to persevere and believe in yourself.

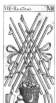

EIGHT

A very busy, hectic time in which you can achieve a great deal. Travel may be indicated.

NINE

Not a good time to take risks. Draw on your self-belief, courage and strength of purpose.

TEN

You feel overwhelmed by a burden and unable to see the way forward. Delegate or rethink your options.

PAGE

An exciting and stimulating phase involving a journey or interesting enterprise is indicated.

KNIGHT

This indicates a restless and exhilarating time in which you are eager to make changes and see what you can achieve.

QUEEN

You'll either encounter someone who is enthusiastic and warm or you need to cultivate these qualities yourself.

KING

Take charge of your life and develop your entrepreneurial and creative abilities.

THE SUIT OF PENTACLES

Pentacles rule practical and materialistic concerns, including day-to-day work, money, property, possessions, and business deals. They correspond to Diamonds in playing cards, and in Western astrology to the three Earth signs of Taurus, Virgo, and Capricorn.

ACE

A change of career or a new job, the start of a business venture, or a financial project, or the arrival of money may be signified.

FOUR

You feel stuck and unable to move forward because you are reluctant to take risks and disrupt the status quo.

TWO

Balance your finances or juggle your time and energy. Consider how you can improve the situation.

FIVE

Don't become so wrapped up in your current difficulties that you lose sight of what is worthwhile.

THREE

You have carried out the groundwork on a financial or material project and you now need to move on to the next step.

SIX

Either money is on the way to you or you'll be giving money to someone else. There can also be a sense of lack.

SEVEN

Are you making the best use of your skills and abilities? You may be overlooking a valuable talent.

EIGHT

It's a good opportunity to develop a new skill, especially if this means retraining or taking on an apprenticeship.

NINE

This card represents contentment through hard work or material stability, or making money from the land.

TEN

Financial or business prosperity is indicated, or a strong and stable family life. Sometimes this card indicates a happy house move.

PAGE

This may indicate a small windfall or a talent that you can develop into a secure income or successful career.

KNIGHT

This could represent a dependable, reliable person or a situation that has become bogged down in stalemate or a rut.

QUEEN

Either someone who is practical or the need for you to pay more attention to your material comforts is indicated.

KING

This represents either someone who is experienced in business and finance, or the need for you to count your blessings.

THE SUIT OF SWORDS

Swords are linked with the difficulties that we face in life and the worries that often arise as a result. They rule words, ideas, decisions, and opinions. Swords correspond to Spades in playing cards, and in Western astrology to the three Air signs of Gemini, Libra, and Aquarius.

ACE

This represents the birth of an exciting concept, the need to reach a decision, or an idea that dominates your thoughts.

TWO

The need to face facts and confront your fears is signified. If you don't do this, you'll be stuck in a stalemate.

THREE

Arguments and separations may be indicated, or the need to cut someone out of your life. Sometimes it represents a medical procedure.

FOUR

A time of rest and recuperation may be indicated, whether on a vacation or by retreating from a difficult situation.

FIVE

Accept your limitations, acknowledge the difficulties that you face and don't overstretch yourself.

SIX

Life has been tough but you are now experiencing a period of calm and are heading toward some easier times.

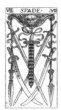

SEVEN

The need for clever tactics and keen diplomatic skills in order to resolve a tricky situation are indicated.

PAGE

The need to study the small print of a contract or agreement is indicated, or to think things through before making a decision.

EIGHT

You are feeling trapped by difficult circumstances that may be self-imposed, and are unable to move beyond them.

KNIGHT

A situation that begins rapidly and may end just as quickly. It could be a time when you have to make snap decisions.

NINE

This indicates a time of great worry and anxiety, often causing sleepless nights. Don't let your fears run away with you.

QUEEN

This represents the ability to learn from experience and cope stoically with whatever life throws at you.

TEN

This may represent a bitter disappointment or the difficult end of a cycle but the chance to start again.

KING

The need to gain an expert opinion in order to solve a difficulty is indicated, or someone who is decisive and authoritative.

THE SUIT OF CUPS

Cups are associated with emotions, relationships, creativity, cherished possessions, memories, and spirituality. Cups correspond to Hearts in playing cards, and in Western astrology to the three Water signs of Cancer, Scorpio, and Pisces.

ACE
The start of a happy situation, a new relationship, the birth of a child, or a spiritual experience are indicated.

TWO
This represents a union or contract, harmony in a relationship, an emotional commitment, or a successful partnership.

THREE
This symbolizes the joys of friendship, a celebration, or the relief that comes after a difficult phase is over.

FOUR
A sense of discontent and the inability to appreciate what is in front of you is indicated, as well as missed opportunities.

FIVE
This represents regret and remorse, or grieving over what's been lost rather than focusing on what has been retained.

SIX
Nostalgia, which may be misplaced, or the reappearance of someone or something from the past is indicated.

SEVEN

You've been presented with so many choices that it's difficult to make the right decision.

EIGHT

A relationship or chapter in your life is over and you must walk away from it toward something new.

NINE

The wish card of the Minor Arcana, indicating that a dream could be realized. Indicates happiness and contentment.

TEN

Success and achievement after a period of struggle or hard work. A happy family life or a successful house move.

PAGE

A spiritual journey or the start of an emotionally fulfilling relationship or enterprise.

KNIGHT

The start of a love affair or spiritually nourishing project. The quest for love on all levels.

QUEEN

This indicates a time to focus on your emotions and deepest needs. The ability to tune into the unseen realms.

KING

The need to become more openly affectionate and demonstrative, to be more approachable is signified.

TAROT SPREADS

When you consult the tarot, you lay out the cards in a particular pattern that is known as a spread. There are many spreads to choose from, according to the question you wish to ask. Below are some classic spreads; you will find other spreads in the section on playing cards (see pages 194–201).

THE HORSESHOE

This is one of the classic spreads. The Horseshoe works well when you want to look at a situation in depth.

1 Past influences
2 The present
3 Hidden influences
4 Obstacles
5 Outside influences
6 The best course of action
7 The outcome

THE CELTIC CROSS

This is another of the classic tarot spreads. It is excellent at giving an overview of a situation.

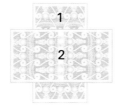

1 Your current position
2 The difficulties you are facing
3 Your current concerns
4 What is passing out of your life
5 Your recent past
6 Your immediate future
7 Your near future
8 The influences around you
9 Your hopes and fears
10 The outcome

THE HOROSCOPE

The horoscope spread enables you to look at 12 areas of your life, and the divisions match the 12 houses of the horoscope. An alternative way to use this spread is to assign one month to each card, starting with the month ahead. It is a particularly good spread to use for the start of the year.

1 Your personal life
2 Values and possessions
3 Communications, short journeys, and siblings
4 Home, family, and roots
5 Children, creativity, and love
6 Health, day-to-day routine, and being of service
7 Relationships
8 Official and shared finances, intense relationships
9 Challenges, education, and long-distance travel
10 Career, social status, and long-term goals
11 Hopes and wishes, friends
12 Secrets and fears

CREATING YOUR OWN SPREADS

If you can't find a suitable spread there is nothing to stop you from creating your own. Simply decide which areas of your life you want to look at (such as money, love, career, and health), or which elements of a situation you want to examine in more detail. Write down what each card will represent to avoid forgetting which category is which when you lay out the spread.

For instance, if you are in two minds about taking a new job, you could devise a suitable spread that gives you insight into each of your options. You can weigh up the consequences of each option.

Options spread

First option
1 Benefits of keeping your current job
2 Drawbacks of keeping your current job
3 Best course of action

Second option
1 Benefits of taking the new job
2 Drawbacks of taking the new job
3 Best course of action

SAMPLE TAROT READING

Edward needs guidance about his career. He has recently become a father for the first time and his wife wants him to get a better-paying job. Something of a hippie at heart, Edward is worried about climbing on to the corporate ladder and eventually becoming a person he neither knows nor likes.

THE SPREAD

The most striking features of this Celtic Cross spread are the number of Pentacles (four), signifying the need for Edward to concentrate on practicalities and money, the two Aces (signifying fresh starts), and the absence of any Major Arcana cards, showing that matters are in his own hands and for him to control.

Edward's current position— Ten of Wands

He is clearly making life difficult for himself and feels that everything is too much of a burden.

The difficulties he's facing— King of Wands

This card represents the innovative go-getter that Edward feels he should become in order to have a successful career.

His current concerns— Four of Pentacles

He is happy with the status quo and reluctant to change it by taking risks.

What's passing out of his life— Seven of Pentacles

Edward feels that he would have to abandon the satisfyingly creative side of his job, signified by this card, for an unfulfilling management role.

His recent past—Seven of Wands

Life is difficult with a new baby and he felt there weren't enough hours in the day. Everything was competing for his time.

His immediate future— Ace of Pentacles

A project promising money is beckoning. It is a good time to start a business venture.

His near future— Queen of Swords

Edward will soon have to examine his high ideals and learn from experience.

The influences around him— Ace of Cups

This card symbolizes his happiness at having a baby daughter and his desire to do everything he can to support his family.

His hopes and fears— Eight of Swords

Edward clearly feels trapped and frightened by the prospect of taking a job he might hate.

The outcome— Eight of Pentacles

Edward is being reminded that he has many talents. He decides to retrain for a job that he will love and which will pay well.

10

3

9

5   **1**   **6**

2

8

4

7

PART SIX

Playing cards

HOW PLAYING CARDS WORK

You may not have a deck of tarot cards at home but it's almost certain that you've got some playing cards hidden in a cupboard or drawer. This makes them one of the most accessible ways to tell fortunes.

There are 52 cards in a deck of playing cards. They are divided into four suits—Clubs, Diamonds, Spades and Hearts. Each suit consists of ten "pip" cards plus three court cards—Kings, Queens, and Jacks or Knaves. Although you may already have a deck of playing cards at home you might wish to buy a special deck that you only use for telling fortunes. This will ensure that the energy it accumulates whenever you use it to give readings isn't dissipated or confused when you use it to play cards.

USING A NEW DECK
If you buy a special deck for fortune telling, you must impregnate it with your energy. The best way to do this is to handle the cards as much as possible. You must also shuffle them very well to mix up their order. Try placing them on a flat surface and move them around with your hands so their order becomes completely random.

USING 52 OR 32 CARDS
You can practice cartomancy, which is the art of fortune telling with playing cards, using the entire deck or a shortened version of 32 cards. When using the entire deck, you follow the same card meanings as those that are given for the Minor Arcana of the tarot (see pages 152–159). However, if you wish to use the 32-card version, you will find the interpretations of these cards in this section.

CHOOSING A SIGNIFICATOR
In cartomancy, it's traditional to choose a card, called a significator, which represents the person for whom the reading is being given. This is always one of the court cards, chosen according to the age and sex of the person concerned. For instance, Kings are always used to represent men, Queens to represent women, and Jacks for young people or children. You can choose from a

Always shuffle the cards properly before dealing
them out, especially if they're brand new.

Spend time handling your playing cards to impregnate them with your energy.

variety of other considerations when selecting the suit, as you can see from the table. Choose one particular category and abide by it during the reading because it will help you to identify the people represented by other court cards that might appear in the reading.

HOW TO PROCEED WITH THE READING

After choosing an appropriate significator, leave that card in the deck and then shuffle it as normal before dealing the cards into a spread. Before you read the cards, look to see if the significator is among them. If that card is to one side of the spread it shows that the person concerned is on the periphery of the situation. Perhaps it's only just starting or it's coming to an end, or maybe the person is feeling dispassionate about what's happening. If the significator is in the middle of the spread, the person is completely involved in the situation.

Look for other court cards that belong to the same suit as the significator because these will indicate people who are connected to the person receiving the reading. The nature of the relationship between the cards is always determined by the nature of the relationship being discussed, so in a reading about someone's career the court cards will represent colleagues, bosses, employees or clients.

For instance, if the significator is the King of Spades and the reading concerns relationships, the Jack of Spades will refer to the significator's child or his thoughts.

CHARACTERISTICS OF SUITS AND CARDS

	Clubs	**Diamonds**	**Spades**	**Hearts**
Birth sign	Aries	Taurus	Gemini	Cancer
	Leo	Virgo	Libra	Scorpio
	Sagittarius	Capricorn	Aquarius	Pisces
Coloring	Brown hair	Fair or red hair	Dark brown or black hair	White or blond hair
	Brown or hazel eyes	Green eyes	Brown eyes	Blue or green eyes
	Ruddy skin	Fair skin, freckles	Dark complexion	Fair skin
Personality	Loyal	Outgoing	Articulate	Emotional
	Trustworthy	Money-minded	Clever	Sensitive
	Enthusiastic	Security-conscious	Objective	Affectionate

CARTOMANCY USING A SHORTENED DECK

If you are new to cartomancy or you are already familiar with the tarot and you'd like to develop a completely different way of working with the cards, this may be the technique for you. It's very simple and, as you will see, the interpretation of each card is fairly short.

However, this technique has a twist because each card's upright position is clearly marked on it, enabling you to expand your interpretations to upright and reversed meanings.

You may be able to buy a set of playing cards where there is a clear difference between the upright and reversed images on the cards, but it's far more likely that you'll have to mark the cards yourself. Make sure that you mark each card in the same way, such as putting a red dot in the top right-hand corner to show that this is the right way up.

CONSTRUCTING THE 32-CARD DECK

When you've chosen the deck you want to use, you must go through it and remove every card between Two and Six inclusive.

This will leave you with the 32-card deck, consisting of eight cards in each suit: the four Aces, plus every card from Seven up to the King. When you take into account the reversed meanings as well, you will have a 64-card deck.

THE SUITS

When using this shortened deck, the meaning of the individual suits is not as important as it is when using the full deck. You will notice, therefore, that the meanings of the cards in the 32-card deck are different from those in the full deck, where the suits play a much greater role in the interpretation of the cards.

COMBINATIONS

Suits may not count for much in the 32-card deck but combinations of cards are considered to be very important. They give an entirely different dimension to the meaning of the cards in a spread.

Mark each card in the same way so you'll know which is its upright position.

♣ CLUBS

Clubs are the equivalent of Wands in the Minor Arcana of the tarot. They correspond to the Fire signs in Western astrology of Aries, Leo, and Sagittarius.

ACE

Good fortune is coming your way. There will also be good news, which could arrive in a letter.

Reversed A letter is coming, but it will bring worrying news.

Combinations If Diamonds are near the card or it is surrounded by Diamonds, the letter will bring money or news of money. If the Nine of Diamonds is nearby, the letter concerns legal matters. With the Ten of Clubs, a lot of money is on the way. With the Ace of Diamonds, a good contract or agreement will be struck.

The Ace of Clubs traditionally indicates letters but could now mean e-mails as well.

KING

This card represents a dark-haired man. He is a good friend, loyal, and trustworthy.

Reversed There is worry or disappointment connected with the man described in the upright position for this card. Plans that you've made may not come to anything.

Combinations When this card appears with the Ten of Clubs, there could be an offer of marriage.

QUEEN

A friendly, dark-haired woman. She's affectionate and loyal, a good person to have on your side.

Reversed There are difficulties connected with the woman described in the upright position. She may arouse someone's jealousy because she's flirtatious or treacherous, or she might have a bad temper and be unpredictable.

Combinations With the Ace of Spades, a difficult journey. With the Seven of Diamonds, the outcome of events is unsure.

JACK

A dark-haired young man. He's good fun and an amusing companion. He may be an ardent lover or a life-enhancing friend. He can also signify the thoughts of the person represented by the King of Clubs.

Reversed This isn't someone you can trust. He may be fickle emotionally or simply foolish. He may also have a good line in meaningless flattery.

Combinations With the Jack of Spades, a difficult working partnership or loss of money and prestige.

TEN

Prosperity and abundance are indicated. There will be happiness and the easy living conditions that come from luxury.

Reversed There could be a journey, either by air or by water. This is still a favorable card when reversed. If there are any problems they will be irritating but fleeting.

With practice you will become quick at shuffling and dealing the cards.

Combinations With the Ten of Spades, there will be a journey overseas. With the Ace of Clubs, a lot of money is on the way. With the Ten of Diamonds, there will be a journey across water.

NINE

Unexpected money, especially as the result of a legacy or inheritance.

Reversed There is the potential for an argument, especially if it's the result of someone's greed or selfish actions.

Combinations With the Eight of Hearts, there will be happiness and a potential celebration. With the Nine of Hearts, a fortunate inheritance.

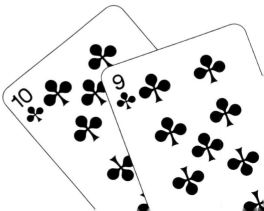

EIGHT

This is a fortunate card, indicating the love of someone who will be beneficial to you. Sometimes this person can be wealthy, important, or influential.

Reversed Avoid any form of speculation or risk because it won't work out in the way you want. Alternatively, there can be problems in a close relationship.

Combinations When this card appears with the Ten of Diamonds, it signifies a journey that will be taken for emotional reasons, such as going to meet a lover. With the Eight of Diamonds, there is true love.

SEVEN

Small amounts of money could come your way, particularly through a modest win or a pay raise. It's also a beneficial card if your question concerns business matters.

Reversed Problems connected with money, such as mounting debts or unexpected bills. Avoid wasting money, effort, or opportunities.

Combinations With the Jack of Hearts, a love affair in which one of the partners is more interested in the material side of the relationship than in the emotional benefits. With the Seven of Diamonds, money will arrive from an inheritance. With the King of Spades, investments should be made with caution and care.

DIAMONDS

Diamonds are the equivalent of Pentacles in the Minor Arcana of the tarot. They correspond to the Earth signs in Western astrology of Taurus, Virgo, and Capricorn.

ACE

This is a very fortunate card and often indicates a gift that will come from a lover or friend. This might be a ring or some other jewelry, perhaps connected with an engagement or marriage. It can also indicate a letter containing positive news.

Reversed Delays connected with letters or money. Sometimes it represents upsetting or worrying news or an unpleasant letter.

Combinations With the Ace of Clubs, a contract or agreement will be struck. When combined with the Ten of Hearts, there will be a love affair and possibly a marriage. With the Jack of Diamonds, someone who will bring money. With the Ace of Hearts, there will be a wedding or commitment.

When the Ace of Diamonds appears with the Ace of Hearts they refer to a forthcoming wedding.

KING

This card represents a man with very fair or possibly even white hair. Traditionally, he's a soldier but equally he might be in charge of other people; perhaps a boss or a leader of some sort. He has strong aims and ambitions.

Reversed There could be deceit or betrayal connected with the man described in the upright position of this card. He likes to scheme in order to get his own way, regardless of how this affects other people.

Combinations When this card is combined with the Eight of Spades there will be an unexpected journey.

QUEEN

This card describes a woman with fair or red hair. She's energetic and outgoing, and has strong powers of intuition.

Reversed There could be gossip or spite from the woman described in the upright position. She can be single-minded and subjective, and also manipulative when she wants to get her own way.

Combinations With the Ace of Spades, there will be a difficult journey. With the Seven of Hearts, there will be happiness, but in contrast possessiveness and jealousy will sometimes cause problems and jeopardize this happiness.

JACK

This often shows the thoughts of the person represented by the King or Queen of Diamonds if they both appear in the same spread. It can also indicate a bright, lively child or a young man, especially if it appears next to a court card. Sometimes, it indicates an employee or someone who's in a lowly position.

Reversed Someone who can't be trusted, perhaps because he's deceitful or simply because he doesn't know his own mind. This card can also represent someone who hasn't yet found the right niche in life and is still searching for their path.

Combinations With the Ace of Diamonds, someone who will bring money in near by. With the Nine of Spades, care should be taken when listening to the advice of friends or colleagues.

TEN

Some form of travel is indicated, such as a vacation, journey, or even a change of residence. This card can also suggest the start of a new cycle in life, and gives reassurance that this will go well and will be successful.

Reversed When reversed, this card brings delays to the events described in its upright meaning. Things will work out eventually, but they will take their time. Sometimes it can indicate a reluctance to accept necessary change.

Combinations With the Ten of Hearts, a nice surprise connected with money. With the Ten of Clubs, a journey across water. With the Seven of Spades, there will be a delay of some kind.

NINE

A favorable time of increase and plenty. There can be happy experiences connected with travel, education, or spirituality.

It's an excellent opportunity to broaden your horizons and be adventurous.

Reversed Unexpected problems connected with money, such as a sudden lack of it. You may have to cancel an exciting project because you can't afford it.

Combinations Very favorable with the Nine of Hearts because whatever is wished for will come true. With the Eight of Hearts, there will be long-distance travel.

EIGHT

This card represents a love affair. It could be with a person but it could equally be with an idea, an enterprise or a place.

Reversed Disappointments connected with love, such as not being able to see your

beloved, or a quarrel between you. Sometimes, it can represent love that's rejected or spurned.

Combinations With the Eight of Hearts, there will be new clothes. With the Eight of Clubs, there is true love.

SEVEN

Minor problems at home or work, especially if these are caused by misunderstandings or pettiness. Happily, these problems will soon be resolved.

Reversed Difficulties and serious problems, particularly involving damage to someone's reputation and prestige.

Combinations With the Queen of Clubs, the outcome of an event isn't certain. With the Seven of Clubs, money will arrive from an inheritance.

The upright Seven of Diamonds indicates fleeting problems with others at work.

SPADES

Spades are the equivalent of Swords in the Minor Arcana of the tarot. They correspond to the Air signs in Western astrology of Gemini, Libra, and Aquarius.

ACE

A powerful or exciting idea that monopolizes the person's thoughts. This card can also indicate the need to make a serious decision.

Reversed A one-track mind caused by an idea or project that becomes an obsession. This card can also suggest unhappiness and bad news.

Combinations With the Queen of Diamonds, there will be a difficult journey. With the Four of Hearts, the birth of a child. With a King or a Jack, the two cards represent a man in uniform or who works for the government. With the Nine of Spades, someone will be very untrustworthy and unreliable. With the Eight of Spades, there will be disappointments.

KING

A man with dark hair and a dark complexion. This card can also indicate a widower, a man who lives alone, or an older man. In addition, it can represent a man who's an expert in his field, such as a lawyer or a surgeon.

Reversed A man who's difficult, authoritarian, or who abuses the trust that others have placed in him. Very occasionally it can represent a man who is malicious and wants to cause trouble.

Combinations With the Seven of Clubs, investments should be made with caution.

QUEEN

A woman with dark hair and a dark complexion. She might be a widow, fairly old, or she may live by herself. Whatever her domestic arrangements, she's had a difficult life and as a result has learnt forbearance and inner strength. She may be rather uncompromising and forthright.

Reversed An ill-intentioned or spiteful woman who is a difficult adversary. She likes to stir up trouble.

Combinations With the Jack of Spades, a woman who is scheming and malevolent.

JACK

A young, dark-haired man with a dark complexion. He may possibly be a student studying law or medicine. He is witty and clever with words, but may also have a sharp tongue.

Practice handling and laying-out the cards to become familiar with them.

Reversed A young man who may mean well but who causes mischief and problems nonetheless. Sometimes, this card can represent a young man who is deceitful and someone to avoid.

Combinations With the Jack of Clubs, a difficult working partnership or loss of money. With the Queen of Spades, a woman who is scheming and malevolent.

TEN

This card can give a warning if the recipient of the reading is involved in something that might cause trouble. This card also signifies unhappiness and sorrow, as well as the dramatic ending of a cycle.

Reversed Difficulties will resolve themselves quickly and won't be nearly as problematic as was first feared.

Combinations With the Ten of Clubs, there will be a journey overseas. With the Queen of Hearts, a difficult enterprise that may not work out well.

NINE

An anxious time in which the person will suffer. There can also be bad news on the horizon. However, the problems are unlikely to be as terrible or wide-ranging as the person feared.

Reversed Problems that seem small at first but which develop in severity and complexity. A laissez-faire attitude that backfires through complacency.

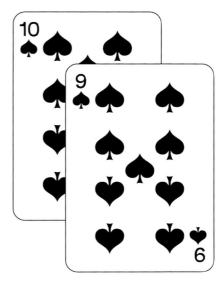

Combinations With the Jack of Diamonds, care should be taken when listening to the advice of friends. With the Ace of Spades, someone will prove to be very untrustworthy and unreliable.

EIGHT

A difficult time in which nothing goes according to plan. A sense of foreboding and the fear that trouble is going to arrive. Worry that the person will repeat past mistakes.

Reversed A love affair that ends badly.

Combinations When combined with the King of Diamonds, there will be an unexpected journey. With the Ace of Spades, there will be disappointments. With the Seven of Spades, a jealous rival who will cause problems.

SEVEN

Problems caused by a member of the family or a friend. The need to seek legal advice if signing a contract or agreement.

Reversed Someone who wriggles out of a difficult situation but causes problems for other people in the process.

Combinations With the Ten of Diamonds, there will be a delay. With the Eight of Spades, there is a jealous rival who will create trouble.

HEARTS

Hearts are the equivalent of Cups in the Minor Arcana of the tarot. They correspond to the Water signs in Western astrology of Cancer, Scorpio, and Pisces.

ACE

Harmony and happiness in the home of the person asking the question or in their immediate surroundings. This card can also indicate joyful news or a love letter.

Reversed A visit from a friend is indicated. Alternatively, this card can suggest a change of residence.

Combinations When surrounded by Hearts, there will be domestic bliss and joy with a special person. With the Ace of Diamonds, there will be a wedding or emotional commitment. With the Jack of Hearts, there will be a proposal.

KING

A man with fair hair and a light complexion. This card can also mean a generous friend who is loyal and helpful, or the promise of some help or a favor.

Reversed A disappointment connected with the man described by this card in the upright position.

Combinations With the Nine of Hearts, there will be a happy love affair leading to a marvelous future.

QUEEN

A woman with fair or light hair, and light skin. She's friendly and affectionate, and someone you can rely on.

Reversed Emotional difficulties with the woman described by this card in the upright position. There could also be problems with a love affair in which this woman is involved.

Combinations With the Ten of Spades, a difficult enterprise that may not work out in the way that was expected.

JACK

The thoughts of the person who is represented by the King or Queen of

Hearts. This card can also describe a young man who is good fun and probably single. Sometimes it can represent a happy child.

Reversed Disappointment connected with a young man.

Combinations With the Seven of Clubs, a love affair in which one of the partners is more interested in the material side of the relationship than in the emotional benefits. With the Ace of Hearts, a proposal.

TEN
This card tells of happiness, good fortune, and enjoyment. It helps to reduce the impact of any neighboring negative cards.

The Ace, King and Queen of Hearts all refer to the joys of friendship and the blessings that come from being with kindred spirits.

Reversed There may be brief problems but they won't amount to much and they will end happily. You'll gain much more than you lose, and the problem concerned may turn out to have been a blessing in disguise.

Combinations When combined with the Ace of Diamonds, there will be a love affair and possibly even an emotional commitment or a marriage. With the Ten of Diamonds, a nice surprise connected with money.

NINE

This is known as the "wish card." Traditionally, it represents the wish of the person for whom the reading is being given, and therefore the neighboring cards will show whether or not the wish will be granted. It can also promise success in whatever is dear to the person's heart at the time of the reading.

Reversed Minor setbacks and brief problems that will soon melt away.

Combinations With the King of Hearts, a happy love affair leading to a marvelous future. With the Nine of Clubs, there will be a fortunate inheritance.

EIGHT

A busy time socially, with plenty of enjoyment. One of these social events may result in meeting a new love. This card can also represent thoughts of emotional commitment, such as marriage.

Reversed Emotional disappointment, perhaps caused by a fickle or inconsiderate lover. Sometimes, it can indicate unrequited love.

Combinations If this card appears with the Nine of Clubs it indicates happiness and a potential celebration. With the Nine of Diamonds, there will be long-distance travel. With the Eight of Diamonds, there will be new clothes.

SEVEN

Enjoyable, happy, and positive thoughts, especially where romance is concerned.

Reversed A relationship that's marred by jealousy and possessiveness.

Combinations With the Queen of Diamonds, there will be happiness but possessiveness and jealousy will cause problems.

GROUPS OF CARDS

In cartomancy, not only do individual cards have meanings that are amplified or altered when two specific cards appear together, but groups of cards also have particular meanings. When you lay out a spread, always check to see if it contains any of the groupings listed here. The cards don't have to fall next to each other, they simply have to appear in the same spread. Here are some of the groupings and what they mean.

Four Aces	A time of major change and fresh starts. Seize the opportunities that are coming your way and don't be afraid of what the future brings.
Three Aces	Good news will arrive after a period of worry.
Two Aces	This describes all forms of partnership. Hearts and Diamonds indicate a successful partnership and possibly a marriage. Diamonds and Spades spell jealousy. Diamonds and Clubs indicate money problems. Hearts and Spades indicate a bitter disappointment. Hearts and Clubs signify financial success. Spades and Clubs mean personality clashes.
Four Kings	Recognition, good fortune, wealth, and a boost to one's reputation. Each reversed card reduces the benefits of this grouping.

Three Kings	A sense of progress. An important project is about to be started. Each reversed card reduces the benefits of this grouping.
Two Kings	Business alliances that start now will be successful. One reversed card means partial success. Two reversed cards mean failure.
Four Queens	Enjoyable social events. Unpleasant gossip if one or more is reversed.
Three Queens	Visitors and women friends. If one or more is reversed, there will be tittle-tattle.
Two Queens	An enjoyable meeting with a friend. The exchanging of confidences. If one or more is reversed, a secret will be betrayed.
Four Jacks	A raucous, fun-filled party. The more cards that are reversed, the more unruly the gathering.
Three Jacks	Problems with friends. The more cards that are reversed, the more unsettled the situation.
Two Jacks	Some form of loss, possibly through a robbery. If both cards are reversed the loss will happen almost immediately.
Four Tens	Tremendous good fortune. However, each reversed card diminishes this.
Three Tens	Difficulties caused by breaking rules or legal problems. Each reversed card reduces the severity of these problems.

Two Tens	An unexpected lucky break. This will arrive immediately if one card is reversed but will be delayed if both are reversed.
Four Nines	A lovely surprise. The more cards that are reversed, the sooner the surprise will arrive.
Three Nines	Very favorable, showing prosperity, success, and good health. The more cards that are reversed, the more there will be brief worries at first.
Two Nines	A modest gain or a successful business connection. If one or both cards are reversed, there will be worries and snags to deal with.
Four Eights	New work or a journey. Reversed cards indicate delays.
Three Eights	A good time to make any sort of commitment. Reversed cards indicate emotional disappointments.
Two Eights	A brief love affair or flirtation. One or both reversed indicates disappointments.
Four Sevens	Difficulties and snags caused by plots and conspiracies. The more cards that are reversed, the more these intrigues are likely to fail.
Three Sevens	Minor illness and a lack of energy. The more cards that are reversed, the less serious these health concerns will be.
Two Sevens	An enjoyable social phase. If one or both cards is reversed, there will be regrets.

OTHER GROUPINGS

A collection of court cards	Happiness, conviviality, and many enjoyable social events.
One court card between two pip cards of the same value	The person represented by the court card is having problems and possibly legal troubles.
A collection of Clubs	Happiness and success.
A collection of Diamonds	Money changing hands.
A collection of Hearts	Love and social events.
A collection of Spades	Worries and problems.

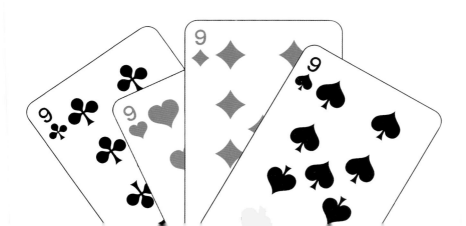

PLAYING CARD SPREADS

Here are some classic cartomancy spreads for you to use, either with the shortened deck or the full 52-card deck. You can also use the spreads given in the tarot section (see pages 160–163).

THE FOUR ACES SPREAD

This is a great way of discovering whether your wish will come true. Using the complete deck for this spread, choose the court card that signifies you or the person for whom the reading is being given and leave it in the deck. Remove the four Aces and arrange them face-up in a cross, with the Ace of Clubs at the top, the Ace of Spades at the bottom, the Ace of Hearts on the left and the Ace of Diamonds on the right. Shuffle the remaining cards well, make a wish, then deal out the cards face-down on to the four Aces.

Examine each set of cards:

• If the Nine of Hearts (the wish card) is in the same set as the significator, the wish will come true.

• With the Eight of Spades as well, there will be delays.

• With the Nine of Spades, there will be an obstacle to the wish.

• If the significator and wish card are with the Ace of Diamonds, the wish will have a financial outcome.

• If they are in the Ace of Hearts set, the wish will have a romantic outcome.

• If they are in the Ace of Clubs set, the wish will have a business outcome,

• If they are in the Ace of Spades set, there will be worries connected with the wish.

If the significator appears without the wish card, look at the surrounding cards. Mostly Hearts and Diamonds show that the wish may come true but there will be delays. Mostly Clubs also show that the wish could come true, but mostly Spades suggest that the wish won't be granted.

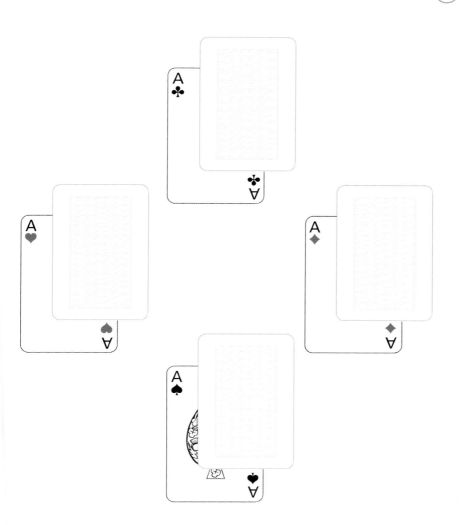

THE MYSTICAL NINE SPREAD

This is an excellent spread for exploring what is happening in your life using the 32-card deck. Before you begin, choose the significator that represents you and put it to one side. Shuffle the remaining deck well, then cut the deck into three piles. Rebuild the deck in reverse order, so the topmost pile now becomes the bottom one. Place the significator in the middle of the table and lay out the cards, dealing them from off the top of the deck, in the pattern and order shown in the illustration. You place the ninth card on top of the significator.

Read the spread in three ways: as individual cards, as three vertical columns, and as three horizontal columns. Start by reading each card in turn, according to what it describes.

1 Your state of mind at the time of the reading
2 The circumstances surrounding you
3 Your home and immediate surroundings
4 Your hopes and fears
5 Your options and opportunities
6 What you want to achieve
7 The difficulties you are facing
8 The strengths on which you can draw
9 Your potential and the future

The card in the ninth position is especially important as it shows how you can make the most of your potential. When you have read the individual cards, you then read the cards horizontally. The top row describes the future. The second row shows the present, and the bottom row describes the past.

Finally, read the vertical columns. The left-hand column describes your character. The central column describes the pitfalls that you must look out for, and the right-hand column describes the decisions you must take.

The future

| 1 | 2 | 3 |

The present

Your character

| 4 | Pitfalls 9 | Decisions to take 5 |

The past

| 6 | 7 | 8 |

SAMPLE CARD READING

Here is a sample reading for Ben using the 32-card deck and a spread known as the Wheel of Fortune.

Ben wanted an overview of his life, which he felt was at crisis point. Rather than ask a specific question of the cards, he wanted to see what they had to tell him.

THE SPREAD

In this spread, the cards are arranged in nine sets of three cards, with each set read in combination to tell a story. After the cards known as the indicators are read, each set of three cards is interpreted. They each describe a point in the future, with the first set describing the immediate future and the eighth set describing the distant future.

SIGNIFICATOR AND INDICATORS

The first step was to choose a significator for Ben. The King of Clubs was the most suitable, as he was in his forties with light brown hair. It was removed from the deck, which Ben then shuffled well. Ben then cut the deck into three piles and turned over each one to reveal the bottom card. These three cards are known as the indicators and were arranged face-up on the table in a row, taking care to keep them in their upright or reversed positions. They indicate general predictions for the future. Ben then reassembled the deck and shuffled it well.

The indicators

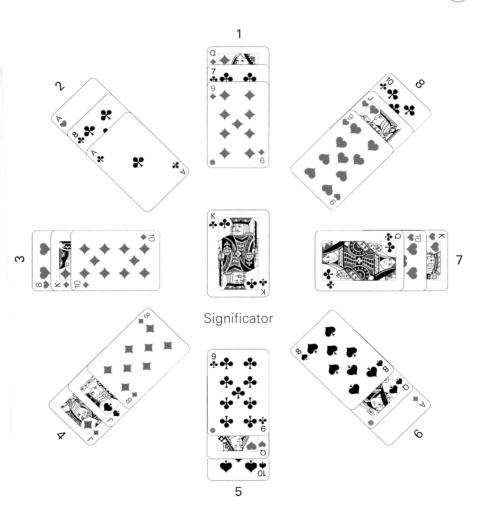

1

2

3

8

7

Significator

4

5

6

DEALING THE CARDS

Next, the significator was placed face-up in the center of the table and eight cards were dealt face-down in a circle around it, working counterclockwise from the position immediately above the significator. Once this circle was complete, another eight cards were laid counterclockwise on top of the first set of cards, also face-down, followed by a third set. The remaining cards were put to one side.

Each set of three cards was turned over and then read, starting with the first set directly above the significator.

The indicator cards

The Seven of Diamonds, the Nine of Spades, and the reversed Jack of Clubs: minor problems and anxiety triggered by an unreliable young man.

The first spoke of the wheel

The Queen of Diamonds, the reversed Seven of Clubs, and the reversed Nine of Diamonds: unexpected money problems connected with a woman with red hair.

The second spoke of the wheel

The Ace of Hearts, the reversed Eight of Clubs, and the Ace of Clubs: financial success yet Ben should avoid taking unnecessary risks.

The third spoke of the wheel

The reversed Eight of Hearts, the King of Diamonds, and the Ten of Diamonds: travel or a fresh start in life, initiated by a strong-willed man, will be successful but could involve unrequited love.

The fourth spoke of the wheel

The reversed Jack of Diamonds, the Jack of Spades, and the Eight of Diamonds: there will be some form of loss, especially if it's connected with a love affair. It may involve a young man who hasn't yet found his path in life.

The fifth spoke of the wheel

The Ten of Spades, the reversed Queen of Hearts, and the reversed Nine of Clubs: arguments triggered by someone's greed will lead to problems in a love affair, which may end in a dramatic fashion.

The sixth spoke of the wheel

The Ace of Diamonds, the reversed Queen of Spades, and the Eight of Spades: Ben

will worry about repeating past mistakes in a love affair but all will go very well provided that he's wary of a woman who could cause trouble.

The seventh spoke of the wheel

The King of Hearts, the reversed Ten of Hearts, and the Queen of Clubs: brief problems with a woman who is close to Ben will melt away, helped by a generous friend.

Place the significator in the center of the table and deal eight cards in a circle around it.

The eighth spoke of the wheel

The reversed Ten of Clubs, the Jack of Hearts, and the Nine of Hearts: everything works out well in the end, with Ben's wishes being granted and much prosperity and happiness.

PART SEVEN

Palmistry

HOW PALMISTRY WORKS

Palmistry is the art of reading your fortune from your hands. Every feature of your hands is taken into account, including their size and shape, their firmness or lack of it, the length of your fingers, the patterns of your fingerprints, the flexibility of your hands, the strength of your thumbs, the shape, size and color of your fingernails, and, last but by no means least, the lines on your palms.

The lines of the palm have great significance in palmistry.

Although you might imagine that the lines on your palm are dictated by the way your hands crease, you'll realize that this isn't entirely true. If you close up your hand you'll see that although some lines definitely correlate to the way your palm creases, others don't have any bearing on this at all. The more lines you have on your palm, the more this will be apparent.

THE PALMISTRY ESSENTIALS

This section gives you a good introduction to palmistry, teaching you some of the basics, including the meaning of the different hand shapes and the major lines of the hand. If you become intrigued by palmistry, there are many books dedicated to this fascinating art.

CAREFUL OBSERVATION

You can, however, also learn a great deal about palmistry by simply observing the people around you. Armed with the basic knowledge that you gain from this section, you'll be able to observe the hands of everyone you meet. Even if you don't ask

someone if you can read her palm, you'll still learn a lot about her from careful observation of her hands. Look at her hand shape to see what this says about her character. Does she have long or short fingers? Are her thumbs strong or weak? What about her fingernails? Are they wide, short or long? Do all these features reflect her personality or do some of them come as a surprise? Don't forget to study your own hands, too, but do be honest when accepting what they may say about you.

Practice reading your own palm before attempting to read other people's.

A MAP OF THE HAND

This is a simplified map of the hand, so you can see where the mounts lie in relation to what are called the major lines of the hand.

Further on in this chapter you will see where the so-called minor lines appear on the hand. First take time to familiarize yourself with the layout of the palm, so you are confident about which line is which.

RIGHT OR LEFT?

When you are reading someone's hand, one of the first questions you should ask him is whether he's left- or right-handed. This is very important because it determines which is his dominant hand. This is the hand that rules his present and shows what he's capable of actually doing. His non-dominant hand describes his dreams and his potential. However, he may not necessarily ever put these into practice.

Take time to familiarize yourself with the layout of the palm.

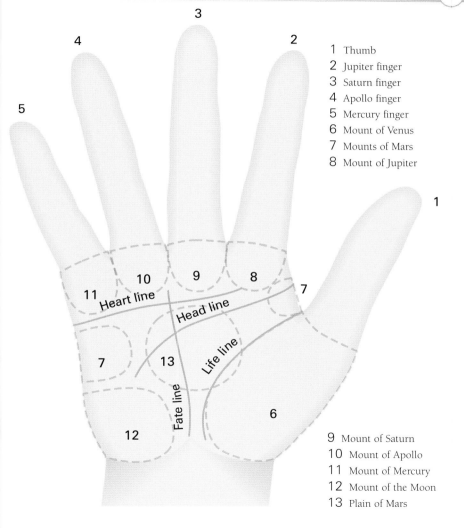

1 Thumb
2 Jupiter finger
3 Saturn finger
4 Apollo finger
5 Mercury finger
6 Mount of Venus
7 Mounts of Mars
8 Mount of Jupiter

9 Mount of Saturn
10 Mount of Apollo
11 Mount of Mercury
12 Mount of the Moon
13 Plain of Mars

THE SHAPE OF THE HAND

Hands are divided into four categories, each based on one of the elements of Western astrology. Sometimes you'll see hands that are a mixture of two types.

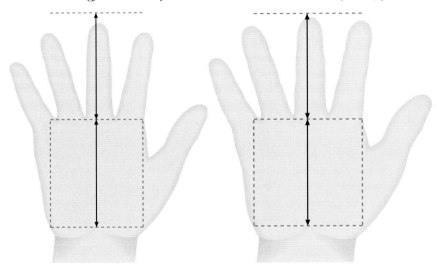

FIRE HAND

This hand has a long palm with fingers that are shorter than the palm. The skin is springy and warm, and both the major and minor lines are clearly visible. Someone with a Fire hand is energetic, enthusiastic, competitive, and lively. She likes to be kept busy but can find it hard to relax.

EARTH HAND

This hand has a square palm and stiff fingers that are shorter than the palm. The skin is thick and the hand feels hard. Often only the major lines are visible. Someone with an Earth hand is practical, straightforward and honest. She has plenty of common sense but may lack imagination.

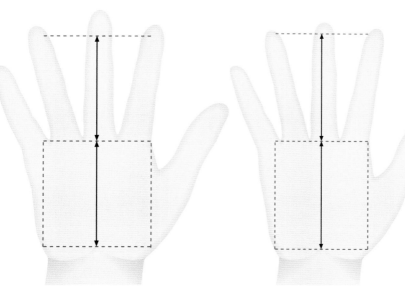

AIR HAND

An Air hand has a square palm with flexible fingers that are longer than the palm. The skin is dry and the hand feels quite soft. The lines are thin but are clearly marked. Someone with an Air hand is intelligent and excels at all forms of communication. It's hard for her to express her emotions.

WATER HAND

A Water hand has a long palm and long, sometimes double-jointed, fingers. The skin is damp and soft, and the palm is covered with lines. Someone with a Water hand is intuitive, compassionate, and emotional. She may also have strong artistic abilities, and she can be gullible and unworldly.

THE MOUNTS

The mounts are arranged around the outside of the palm, as you can see in the diagram. In each case, the more pronounced the mount, the more pronounced the qualities that it describes. Equally, an underdeveloped mount shows that those particular qualities are undeveloped.

THE MOUNT OF VENUS

The focus of this mount is the ability to express emotion and to be demonstrative, as well as general levels of vitality.

THE MOUNT OF JUPITER

This mount expresses ambition, confidence, and leadership ability.

THE MOUNT OF SATURN

Self-control, sense of duty, and responsibility are the focus of this mount.

THE MOUNT OF APOLLO

This mount is devoted to social skills, enjoyment of life, and artistic talents.

THE MOUNT OF MERCURY

Ability to communicate with other people and to express himself are the concerns of this mount.

THE MOUNTS OF MARS

There are two mounts of Mars: the inner mount above the thumb shows physical courage and the outer mount on the side of the hand indicates moral courage.

THE PLAIN OF MARS

This indicates the level of self-confidence.

THE MOUNT OF THE MOON

The mount of the Moon rules imagination and sensitivity.

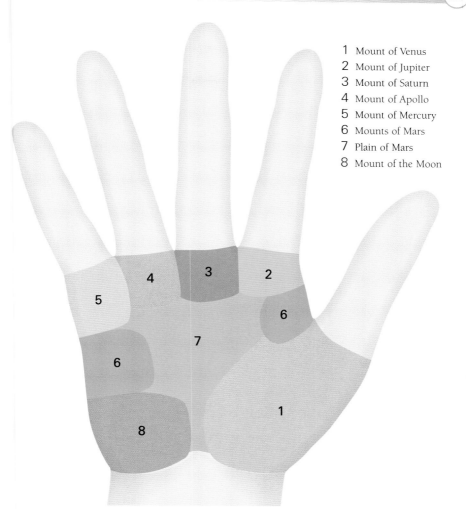

1 Mount of Venus
2 Mount of Jupiter
3 Mount of Saturn
4 Mount of Apollo
5 Mount of Mercury
6 Mounts of Mars
7 Plain of Mars
8 Mount of the Moon

THE FINGERS AND THUMBS

The shape and size of our fingers and thumbs reveal a great deal of information about our character. You will learn a lot about other people simply by observing their thumbs and fingers.

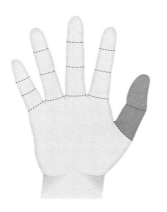

THE THUMB

This digit describes a person's ego, willpower, logic, and motivation. A normal thumb (roughly the same length as the Mercury or little finger) indicates a healthy ego without being over-confident, and good motivation. A long thumb shows that the person is well-organized and skilled at taking charge of situations, sometimes to the point of being over-controlling. A short thumb indicates a weak, submissive, and unmotivated person.

THE JUPITER OR INDEX FINGER

This finger indicates someone's confidence, leadership abilities, and ego. A normal Jupiter finger ends halfway up the top phalange of the Saturn or middle finger. This shows a well-balanced ego and an ability to take the lead when necessary. A long Jupiter finger shows increased self-confidence, possibly leading to egotism and arrogance. When short, this finger indicates shyness and an inability to take the initiative.

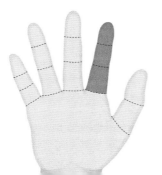

THE SATURN OR MIDDLE FINGER

The middle finger shows our sense of responsibility. A normal Saturn finger is three-quarters the length of the palm, and shows a well-balanced sense of duty and conscientiousness. A long Saturn finger indicates someone who is trustworthy but may take on too much responsibility. When it's short, the person avoids responsibility and struggles to make decisions.

THE APOLLO OR RING FINGER

This finger shows creative ability and emotional responses. A normal Apollo finger is shorter than the Jupiter finger, and it shows someone who's demonstrative, sociable, and has a good artistic sense. A long Apollo finger indicates someone who wears his heart on his sleeve. He's artistic and good company. A short Apollo finger shows an inability to show emotions and a general lack of interest in creative and artistic pursuits.

THE MERCURY OR LITTLE FINGER

The little finger shows someone's ability to communicate and also his level of honesty. A normal Mercury finger reaches the start of the top phalange of the Apollo or ring finger. It shows a normal ability to communicate with others. When it's long, there is a gift for communication, such as writing or public speaking. When it's short, the person can become tongue-tied or very withdrawn.

THE HEART LINE

This line describes a person's ability to connect with her emotions and to express them to others. It also shows the general nature of her relationships, and whether they are happy or difficult. Look at the shape and quality of the line, as well as where it ends. Breaks indicate interruptions to the person's emotional energy.

CURVED OR STRAIGHT HEART LINE?

Deeply curved Highly attuned to other people and very sensitive emotionally.
Curved A warm emotional response to others and a friendly nature.
Straight A lack of sensitivity to others and an inability to express her own emotions.

WHERE DOES IT END?

As you can see from the diagram, the heart line always starts on the outer edge of the hand but can end in one of four places:
Ends under Saturn finger This is considered to be a short heart line and shows a restricted range of emotional responses. She takes her emotions seriously.
Ends between Saturn and Jupiter mounts Emotional depth and loyalty are combined with passion and common sense.
Ends under Jupiter finger Idealism can

cause problems in relationships but there are great emotional reserves.
Ends on the side of the palm This is a very long heart line, showing that the person experiences a wide range of emotions. She may also be demanding, jealous, and emotionally immature.

POSITION ON THE PALM

Look for the position of the line on the palm:
Close to the base of the fingers This person is entertaining and sociable but has a tendency to be idealistic in relationships.
Midway between base of fingers and head line This person has a well-balanced ability to respond to others.
Close to the head line It's hard for this person to express her feelings and be demonstrative with loved ones.

1 Ends under Saturn finger
2 Ends between Saturn
and Jupiter mounts
3 Ends under Jupiter finger
4 Ends on the side of
the palm

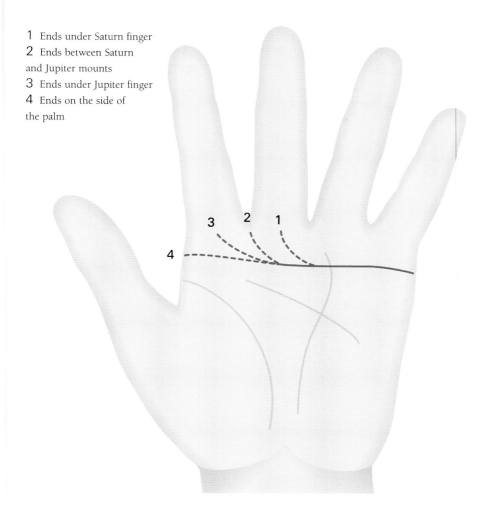

THE HEAD LINE

This line indicates a person's intellect, his ability to think rationally and clearly and to convey his ideas to others. Look at the shape and quality of the line, as well as where it ends. Breaks indicate interruptions to the person's emotional energy.

WHERE DOES IT START AND END?

The head line can begin in three different positions, as you'll see in the diagram, and can end in four different places. Each position has a particular meaning:

Starts on mount of Jupiter This person is confident in his abilities and is ambitious. If there's a big gap between the head line and the life line, it shows that he's independent.

Starts joined to life line This person is cautious and always likes to get a second opinion before making important decisions. His family has a strong influence on him.

Starts below life line Shy and unsure of himself, this person needs tremendous amounts of reassurance from others that he's doing well in life.

Ends beneath Saturn finger This is a very short line, showing a lack of flexibility in thinking. This person expresses himself with seriousness.

Ends beneath Apollo finger This person has artistic flair and enjoys expressing himself creatively.

Ends on mount of Mars beneath Mercury finger This person lacks confidence in himself, and in his intellectual abilities.

Ends on mount of the Moon This ending shows a high degree of imagination but also the potential to be easily depressed.

WRITER'S FORK

Sometimes the head line ends in a fork, which is commonly known as the writer's fork. Although it can indicate writing talent, it really shows an ability to see more than one side to any argument.

SIMIAN LINE

Sometimes the head and heart lines are joined together in a single line known as a simian line. This indicates someone whose thoughts and emotions work together.

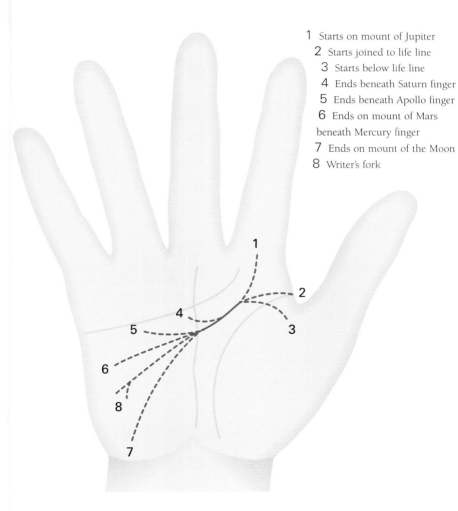

1 Starts on mount of Jupiter
2 Starts joined to life line
3 Starts below life line
4 Ends beneath Saturn finger
5 Ends beneath Apollo finger
6 Ends on mount of Mars beneath Mercury finger
7 Ends on mount of the Moon
8 Writer's fork

THE LIFE LINE

The life line describes a person's life, with all its joys and difficulties. All the major events in life are indicated along this line, as well as the quality of the person's physical energy. As with every other line on the hand, you must examine the life line's color and thickness, and also look for breaks and other interruptions to it.

WHERE DOES IT START?

The life line runs around the base of the thumb but can start and end in a number of different positions.

Starts on mount of Jupiter This indicates someone who is ambitious, driven, and energetic. She has known what she wants to do with her life from an early age.

Starts between index finger and base of thumb This is the normal starting place for the life line. It shows an average amount of ambition and drive.

Starts joined to head line This shows a lack of confidence, and a need to discuss ideas with other people before putting them into action. It can also show someone who is strongly influenced by her family.

Starts close to base of thumb Someone with this feature is far more interested in the practicalities of life than in intellectual pursuits. She isn't very ambitious.

WHERE DOES IT END?

Ends curved around mount of Venus
A happy home life is essential for this person who views it as a safe retreat from the rest of the world.

Ends on mount of Moon This is the sign of a born traveler or of someone who metaphorically moves away completely from the background or area in which she grew up.

CURVATURE OF THE LINE

You must also consider the curve of the line. A line that seems almost straight indicates a lack of emotional generosity toward others and a tendency to be self-centered. A gentle curve shows shyness, sensitivity and emotional reserve. A very wide curve that sweeps out toward the plain of Mars shows generosity, enthusiasm and a great interest in life.

1 Starts on mount of Jupiter
2 Starts between index finger and base of thumb
3 Starts joined to head line
4 Starts close to base of thumb
5 Ends curved around mount of Venus
6 Ends on mount of Moon

THE FATE LINE

The fate line describes the path that a person takes through life. It can show her career, her interests and whether or not her life will run smoothly. Look carefully for breaks in the line, as these will show times of adversity, and for forks, which show new interests. The life line runs up the middle of the palm.

WHERE DOES IT START?

Starts on mount of Venus This person has been strongly influenced by his family and upbringing, possibly making it difficult for him to break free from them in later life. He may well have chosen a career that fulfilled his parents' expectations.

Starts between mounts of Venus and the Moon This indicates a good balance between meeting the expectations of his family and following his own star come what may.

Starts on mount of the Moon Here is someone who has always known what he wants to do with his life and has followed that path, regardless of what other people might expect from him. He is probably creative and innovative.

WHERE DOES IT END?

Ends at head line This is a short line, indicating someone whose ambition and drive peter out early on. He may drift through life after this or might simply switch from a highly demanding job to something that's much more relaxed.

Ends at heart line This person will opt for an easy-going life after he retires. Look for new lines that branch out from the end of the fate line, indicating fresh interests that spring up after retirement.

Ends on mount of Saturn Here is someone who will remain engrossed in his job or his particular interests until he dies. Retirement is something he'll never consider!

Ends on mount of Jupiter Motivated and ambitious, this person knows where he wants to go in life and will never relinquish his goals, no matter how long it takes to achieve them.

1 Starts on mount of Venus
2 Starts between mounts of
Venus and the Moon
3 Starts on mount of the Moon
4 Ends at head line
5 Ends at heart line
6 Ends on mount of Saturn
7 Ends on mount of Jupiter

THE MINOR LINES AND MARKINGS

Although many of the lines on the hand are rather dismissively called "minor lines," this doesn't diminish their importance. Not every hand has every line, especially Earth hands which may have few if any, but when present they add an extra dimension to the hand. In addition to the minor lines you will probably find several random markings on the hand. Here are the most common minor lines and markings that you can expect to find on a hand.

THE LINE OF MERCURY

This starts at the base of the palm and ends below the mount of Mercury. It indicates a person's health. The ideal line is therefore strong and clear, which shows a good constitution. A weak line indicates that the person needs to take good care of his health. A missing line shows good health.

THE LINE OF APOLLO

The line starts near the base of the wrist and ends on the mount of Apollo. A very beneficial line, indicating creativity, self-motivation, and the ability to be happy.

THE LINE OF MARS

This line starts between the life line and thumb, and ends on the mount of Venus. A well-marked line shows a strong, resilient constitution and good powers of recuperation after illness. It's particularly beneficial if the life line isn't very strong because the line of Mars helps to boost its power.

THE RING OF SOLOMON

This curves around the base of the Jupiter finger. The ring of Solomon shows an ability to connect with others instinctively and to communicate with them on a deep level. It's a good indication of counseling skills and also of teaching ability.

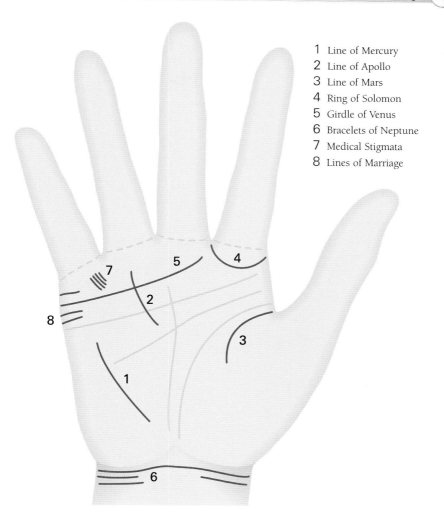

1 Line of Mercury
2 Line of Apollo
3 Line of Mars
4 Ring of Solomon
5 Girdle of Venus
6 Bracelets of Neptune
7 Medical Stigmata
8 Lines of Marriage

THE GIRDLE OF VENUS

The line runs horizontally between the heart line and the base of the fingers. The girdle of Venus denotes a flirtatious, charming, and emotionally sensitive nature. A very strong, unbroken girdle shows someone who is driven by his emotions and can struggle to be faithful. It's better to have a broken girdle of Venus, which shows a less moody, emotionally turbulent character.

THE BRACELETS OF NEPTUNE

You'll find these at the base of the hand, beneath the mounts of Venus and the Moon. These lines are traditionally believed to indicate luck, whereas contemporary palmistry assigns them to health. Either way, at least strong, unbroken bracelets are a good sign. Weak, wavering bracelets suggest delicate health.

THE MEDICAL STIGMATA

Look for a few small, vertical lines on the mount of Mercury; these are the medical stigmata. They indicate an ability and a readiness to help others, traditionally through one of the healing professions. However, if similar lines appear on each mount, those on the mount of Mercury are not medical stigmata.

THE LINES OF MARRIAGE

The lines are located on the side of the hand, between the base of the Mercury finger and the start of the heart line. Traditionally, these lines denoted marriages but today they are more likely to indicate serious relationships. Each line describes a relationship that has a major impact on the person. The stronger the line, the more impact the relationship has.

TRIANGLES

Found along the head line, these show training and education, especially in some form of technical ability. Only concentrate on strongly marked triangles and ignore any that are vague or weak.

SQUARES

These have a protective function, helping to guard against the negative aspects of the area of the palm in which they're found. When they surround a break in a line, they help to mitigate the disruption created by this break.

STARS AND CROSSES

These are both difficult markings. Stars indicate shocks, unless they appear on the mount of Apollo when they mean artistic success. Crosses represent obstacles and other problems that must be overcome.

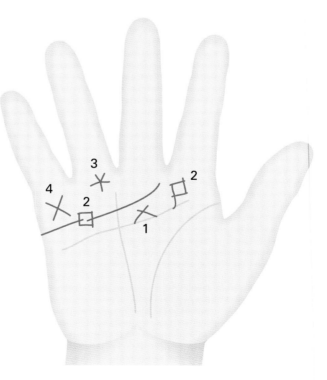

1 Triangle
2 Square
3 Star
4 Cross

PART EIGHT

The I Ching

HOW THE I CHING WORKS

Dating back thousands of years, the I Ching is a simple divination system that originated in China. Yet despite its apparent simplicity, it always goes directly to the heart of the questions you pose, giving you concise and sharp-pointed answers.

THE TRADITIONAL I CHING

Because the I Ching was written in ancient China, much of its traditional language, phraseology, and references sound strange to our 21st-century ears. Translations of the original text speak of a way of life that has long since vanished, so the interpretations given on the following pages have a more contemporary tone that is easier to understand.

Originally, the I Ching was cast using 50 yarrow stalks but that is no longer a popular option because it is so unwieldy. It's far easier to cast the I Ching using three

The I Ching was once thrown using a set of 50 yarrow sticks, but these are rarely used now.

coins, provided that their two sides clearly differ from one another: these are called the inscribed and reversed faces.

Each of the two faces has a different value. The coins are thrown six times, and on each occasion you add up the value of the coins and draw a line—either solid or broken—that corresponds with that value. In this way you build up a hexagram. When this is complete, you refer to the table of trigrams on pages 233 to find the number of this hexagram, and you then look that up in the following pages.

CONSULTING THE I CHING

When you want to ask the I Ching a question you must phrase it in such a way that it can be easily answered. Avoid any either/or questions, such as "Should I buy a new car or put the money in the bank?" because the I Ching will struggle to answer. Instead, divide the question into two halves and then compare the answers you receive. It can also be helpful to ask for insight or guidance about a particular topic, as this opens up the scope of the answer. For instance, you could ask "Will I get a new job soon?" but the answer may not be as informative and helpful as it would be if you asked "Please give me insight into my current job options."

When you've chosen a suitable question, write it on a sheet of paper or in a special divination notebook. You might like to add the time and date so you can keep track of when you asked the question. Writing down the question helps to fix it in your mind and prevents you changing it if you don't like the answer.

THROWING THE COINS

When you're ready to ask your question, study the three coins and decide which side is the inscribed face (usually the one showing the denomination of the coin) and which is the reversed. Make sure you have on hand a pen plus the paper on which you wrote your question.

It is now time to throw the coins. You can either cup them in your hands or shake them in a small container. Shake the coins while thinking of your question, then throw them on to a flat surface. Study the faces of the coins and add up their values to find the total value of that throw. An inscribed face is worth two and a reversed face is worth three. If your total is an even number, it's a yin number which is drawn

as a broken line. If the total is
an odd number, it's a yang
number and is drawn as a
solid line.

Inscribed face = 2
Reversed face = 3

Even number = broken yin line

Odd number = solid yang line

The first throw of the coins
gives you the bottom or sixth
line of the hexagram. The
second throw gives you the fifth
line, and so on. Always draw
the hexagram from the bottom
up until you have completed
the first or top line.

*After shaking the coins throw them
onto a flat surface.*

TABLE OF TRIGRAMS

Consult this table of trigrams to discover the name and number of the hexagram that you've drawn.

Mentally split the trigram into two, and look for the bottom three lines of the trigram on the left-hand side of the page, in the vertical column. Now look for the top three lines of the trigram along the horizontal column. The point where these two trigrams intersect in the table is the number of the hexagram you've drawn. For instance, if the bottom trigram consists of three broken lines (known as *K'un*) and the top trigram consists of three solid lines (known as *Ch'ien*), the hexagram's number is 12.

You can use any coins you wish. Alternatively, you could use three classic I Ching coins.

	Chien	Chên	K'an	Kên	K'un	Sun	Li	Tui
Chien	1	34	5	26	11	9	14	43
Chên	25	51	3	27	24	42	21	17
K'an	6	40	29	4	7	59	64	47
Kên	33	62	39	52	15	53	56	31
K'un	12	16	8	23	2	20	35	45
Sun	44	32	48	18	46	57	50	28
Li	13	55	63	22	36	37	30	49
Tui	10	54	60	41	19	61	38	58

THE HEXAGRAMS

Here are the interpretations of the 64 hexagrams. Their traditional Chinese name is given as well as an English translation.

1

CH'IEN CREATIVITY

This is a very powerful hexagram because it consists of six unbroken yang lines. It tells you that you are doing well and that if you persevere in the course that you are currently taking you will achieve success. Make yourself strong in every way and don't waste your time on activities that are degrading or not worth the effort. Creative ventures will be especially successful.

2

K'UN DEVOTION

This hexagram is formed from six broken yin lines and therefore it has a yielding quality. Its message is that you'll be successful in your achievements, provided that you don't wander from the path that has been laid out for you. It's better to work with others who can help you to develop your talents than to strike out on your own. Persistence eventually leads to success.

3

CHUN A DIFFICULT BEGINNING

Plants struggle to emerge from the earth but then grow strongly. In the same way, you encounter initial problems with a project before it starts to develop. Be patient and don't be tempted to change direction. Instead, continue on your current course because it will lead to success. It may be wise to ask for assistance or advice.

4

MÊNG INEXPERIENCE

Someone is in need of your advice and the benefit of your wisdom gained from experience. You will be willing to help this person once, but will lose faith and interest in him if he fails to persevere in what he's trying to do or if he becomes too dependent on your assistance. The I Ching also warns not to consult it too often for answers.

5

HSÜ CHOOSING YOUR MOMENT

This isn't the time to rush into things hastily and without planning ahead. Instead, you must bide your time and wait for the right moment before taking action, to ensure that success will follow. When you do take action, you must do so with strength and determination, conserving your energy by not wasting it on needless activities. Choosing the right time to act will lead to great success.

6

SUNG CONFLICT

You are facing difficulties and are caught in a struggle. Even though you may feel that you are in the right, you mustn't insist on getting your own way. Your best course of action is to be ready to compromise and to meet others halfway whenever possible. This will be far more productive in the long run than holding out for what you want, which will only lead to further conflict.

7

SHIH THE ARMY

This is a time when you should take firm action and show that you are in control of the situation and that you are a good leader. People will listen to you if you do this and will abide by what you say. However, abusing your position of power, whether by being dictatorial or self-centered, will turn others against you. Make sure that you play fair with people and then all will be well.

8

PI WORKING IN UNISON

Teamwork is the most productive and effective way to move forward, so do your best to work in tandem with others. If you aren't already part of a team, don't waste any time in assembling a group of people with whom you can collaborate. You can consult the I Ching again if you want to know whether you'll be in a leadership role or one of the group of workers.

9

HSIAO CH'U RESTRAINT

You are gradually moving toward your goals but you haven't attained them yet even though you are starting to glimpse them on the distant horizon. Don't be hasty or charge full steam ahead. Instead, you must exercise restraint, be flexible and understanding with others, and hold yourself back for the time being. This will result in much more success in the long run.

10

LÜ TREADING CAREFULLY

Life may be difficult and you might have to deal with some troublesome or even dangerous people, but you'll be successful if you take things very gently and don't step out of line. You must also be prepared to play by the rules and do nothing that will harm your reputation, despite the provocative behavior of the people around you. Be polite and do your best to keep your sense of humor.

11

T'AI PEACE

Problems, challenges, obstacles, and other difficulties are starting to fade away and will eventually disappear altogether, leaving you in a much more peaceful state of mind. Traditionally, this hexagram is said to represent the fusion of Heaven (the lower trigram) and Earth (the upper trigram), when life becomes much more joyful. The eventual outcome of this hexagram is happiness, success, and prosperity.

12

P'I STAGNATION

You are facing a stalemate in which no progress can be made. People who are weak-willed and caught up in trivial concerns are blocking the way, making it difficult for anyone to succeed. They can't cope with the situation as it stands and as a result are making life difficult for everyone concerned. Your best option may be to retreat from the entire situation before it gets any worse.

13   T'UNG JÊN   FELLOWSHIP

Working with others toward the achievement of shared humanitarian goals is the best way forward. However, you must put your ego to one side because this is no time to be selfish or egocentric. If you work in close harmony with other people you'll be able to weather many storms together. It's a good time to concentrate on activities that will benefit the general public.

14   TA YU   WEALTH

This is a very favorable hexagram because it indicates that wealth, progress, and success will soon be yours. You will experience many different forms of abundance, including financial prosperity and rich relationships. No matter how successful or wealthy you become, you'll avoid developing an inflated ego or thinking that you are more important than everyone around you.

15

CH'IEN MODESTY

Don't let success go to your head. It's important to retain a sense of modesty and humility, and not to believe that you are what you own or what you do for a living. Becoming pompous, pretentious, or self-satisfied will diminish your popularity, so make sure that you remain well-grounded and not swept away by a sense of overweening self-importance.

16

YÜ ENTHUSIASM

This is a good time to enlist the help and support of people who will aid your cause. The best way to do this is to arouse their enthusiasm and energy, so they'll willingly give you their help and will want you to do well. Show them the way forward by being enthusiastic and optimistic yourself. It's a particularly good time to gain the support and backing of a workforce.

17

SUI FOLLOWING

You must follow where your conscience leads you and behave in the way you instinctively know is best. There will be no hardship in this because you'll know that you are doing the right thing. Other people will respond favorably to you because they'll appreciate the way you are behaving. However, bad behavior will mean that people are wary of you and don't trust you.

18

KU DECAY

Past actions have led to mistakes and difficulties that you must now sort out. If you leave them, the situation will only get worse and eventually you won't be able to salvage it. Don't be too quick to repair the damage. Spend three days contemplating what must be done before you take any action, and then devote the following three days to making sure the problems don't arise again.

19

LIN MAKING PROGRESS

You are making good progress and will continue to do so for the time being. Make the most of this fortunate time by working with determination and perseverance. Seize opportunities whenever you find them and maintain a positive, constructive attitude. However, nothing lasts forever and this propitious phase will eventually be overtaken by more difficult circumstances.

20

KUAN CONTEMPLATION

This is an excellent time to set a good example to others by behaving in a dignified and sincere manner, and especially by remembering the spiritual law of cause and effect. People will respect you for this. You must also remember that life runs in a continuous cycle of growth followed by decay, and that it's a pointless exercise to fight against this natural order.

21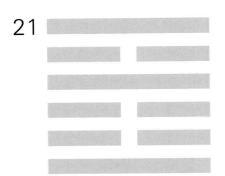

SHIH HO BITING THROUGH

You need to bite through whatever is holding you back or causing problems for you at the moment, and one way to do this is through a legal process, especially if the problems are extremely severe. But you must combine gentleness with determination while doing this, as one without the other won't work properly. Face up to whatever must be done.

22

PI BEAUTY

Beauty and adornment have their place in life but you must know when they are not appropriate. For instance, when you are making plans you must take care not to be sidetracked by unimportant details that have little real value. This is a good time to take greater care over your image or to enhance it in some way, provided that you don't give it too much significance.

23

PO SPLITTING APART

Something, such as a relationship or circumstance, is in the process of falling apart and disintegrating. This has happened as a result of a long period in which the relationship or situation has been undermined by forces that it can't withstand. There is nothing that you can do to change this because it's part of the natural cycle of life. However, you can accept the situation with grace and composure.

24

FU THE TURNING POINT

This is the turning point after a period of decay, similar to the time of the winter solstice when the days gradually begin to lengthen. Things begin to move again and they do so without the need to force them. They happen of their own accord at their own pace. You now start to feel that situations are working in your favor and that you will be successful again.

25

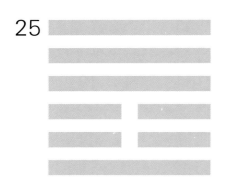

WU WANG HONESTY

It is essential to be honest and to behave with integrity and honor. If you don't do this, you'll encounter many difficulties and won't be able to make any progress at all. But if you are straightforward and behave correctly, you will be able to enjoy great success and influence. Do your best not to judge others or to be prejudiced in any way. Instead, be open-minded and fair to everyone you meet.

26

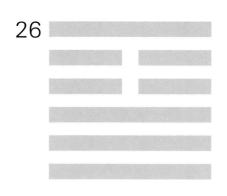

TA CH'U GAINING THROUGH RESTRAINT

This is a good time to restrain your impulses and to act in a correct manner. Doing this will help to ensure success and progress. This is also an excellent time for any form of travel, because widening your social circle and mixing with people that you wouldn't normally meet will bring you increased good fortune and understanding. You may meet someone who has a position of power.

27

I GAINING NOURISHMENT

There are many forms of nourishment, including physical, emotional, and spiritual. Consider how you can nourish the people around you as well as yourself, and give everyone the nourishment that is appropriate to their needs and desires. Good timing is essential in this, so be sure to help people exactly when they need it. Be moderate when satisfying your own needs.

28

TA KUO EXCESS

You are facing an extreme and stressful situation that will quickly lead to some form of disaster or collapse unless you can take avoiding action very soon. You may feel that a situation has reached breaking point and that you can't tolerate it any longer. Whatever is wrong, it might help to confide in someone you trust or to ask him for help. This person may have expert knowledge.

29

K'AN THE ABYSS

This is a difficult time for you when you are facing many difficulties. You may even be struggling with one problem after another. Take firm action and keep your end goal in sight in order to succeed. It's essential for your peace of mind that you realize the difference between the difficulties that you can master and overcome, and those that are completely beyond your control.

30

LI FIRE

Allow the true beauty of your nature to unfold, no matter what the circumstances are that you are facing. You are dependent on many things in your life and you must recognize this fact. You will only gain happiness by placing your absolute trust in the workings of universal law, and by believing that everything is happening to you in exactly the way it should. All is well.

31

HSIEN ATTRACTION

There is a powerful current of attraction flowing between you and a certain person. This is a very favorable relationship and, provided that you act in good faith, things will go very well between the two of you and your partnership will be successful. This hexagram is an especially good indication of a forthcoming marriage or a deep emotional commitment to one another.

32

HÊNG DURATION

Success will be yours if you can be resolute and if you behave in ways that are correct, honorable and appropriate to the situation. It will pay to continue with the current situation and not to falter because you will eventually be successful. This is the hexagram of the long haul and of perseverance. Continue with your plans and concentrate on finally achieving them.

33

TUN RETREAT

It would be a wise move to retreat. There is no point in moving ahead with major projects at the moment because they won't make any progress. Nevertheless, you must choose exactly the right time to withdraw in order to retain your dignity and reputation. Concentrate on small enterprises instead because they will do much better for you at the moment.

34

TA CHUANG STRENGTH

You have great strength of purpose but you must use it carefully and with consideration toward others. Don't insist on having everything your own way, nor should you behave improperly because such actions will backfire on you. The means don't justify the ends. If you make the most of your current strength and you combine this with good behavior, you'll have many insights into the workings of the universe.

35

CHIN PROGRESS

This is a time of great progress and achievement for you, and it will happen more quickly than you expected. People in positions of power and influence may grant you favors and will certainly treat you with respect. It's a particularly good time to work for the welfare of others as well as for yourself, and you'll receive many rewards in return for your efforts.

36

MING I QUENCHING OF THE LIGHT

You need to maintain an air of modesty and not to push yourself forward too much. This is especially true if you're dealing with someone who is easily intimidated. You may be more competent than this person but it's not a good time to show it. Instead, you should put your ambitions to one side for the moment, while privately being aware of how much you're capable of achieving.

37

CHIA JÊN THE FAMILY

It's important to do whatever is expected of you within your family or within a particular group to which you belong. Don't step outside the boundaries and do something for which you aren't equipped or which will upset others, even if you know you could do it perfectly well. Success comes from knowing your place and abiding by it, and also by working hard at family life.

38

K'UEI OPPOSITION

You are facing difficulties in a relationship and may even feel as though you are at loggerheads with someone. This can lead to misunderstanding, a lack of trust, and a sense of separation from each other. Don't despair because the situation isn't as hopeless as it seems. Concentrate on achieving small victories with this person, such as laughing together over something.

39

CHIEN OBSTACLES

There are obstacles and problems ahead. Do your best to spot them on the horizon so you are well prepared for them and can find ways to overcome them. However, you may not be able to surmount them by direct means yourself and might have to enlist the help of someone with expert knowledge or tremendous expertise. You'll learn a lot from the experience.

40

HSIEH LIBERATION

Act quickly to avoid problems and to get urgent tasks out of the way. You don't want them hanging over you at the moment and it will be a relief to know that they've been dealt with. This isn't a good time to introduce new ideas and projects, especially if you're only doing so for the sake of change, because they won't go well. Instead, concentrate on the existing arrangements.

41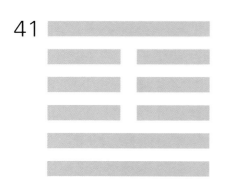

SUN DECREASE

It's a good time to cut back in any area of your life that seems excessive or overblown. This might be your financial expenditure, the number of possessions you own, or your weight. Make any reductions that you know are necessary, even if they're relatively modest. If you need to make sacrifices it will be far better to make small ones willingly than to make big ones that eventually lead to resentment.

42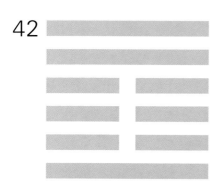

I INCREASE

Everything that you tackle will go well at the moment, but don't wait for too long before taking action because this favorable period won't last forever. This is a particularly good time for any sort of travel. Consider other people in everything that you do and help them when necessary. If you are in a position of authority over others you should act generously toward them.

43

KUAI BREAKTHROUGH

If you've done something wrong, or there are reasons why you should apologize, you must show that your regrets are sincere and heartfelt. You should also be aware of the difficult position in which you've put yourself. This is a good time to be generous toward others. It is also an excellent opportunity to push ahead with an enterprise or venture.

44

KOU ENCOUNTERS

This isn't a good time to embark on any form of committed relationship with someone you have only recently met because you don't know this person as well as you think. You should certainly avoid making a hasty marriage because it won't last long. Watch out for someone who seems insignificant but whose presence starts to cause problems and could eventually lead to disaster.

45

TS'UI GATHERING TOGETHER

It's an excellent time to join together with some of the people in your life, such as family and friends. Things will go well, especially if you are all working together toward a particular goal. It may also help to consult someone who has expert knowledge or the experience that you need. However, be prepared for people to behave in ways you weren't expecting.

46

SHÊNG MOVING UPWARD

You are moving toward success because things are going so well for you. The best way to proceed is to be modest and flexible, rather than to push yourself forward in ways that upset others. Make a start as soon as possible. This is a good time to make contact with people in authority, and if you are going to a job interview you'll be very pleased by what happens.

47

K'UN EXHAUSTION

Don't give up hope, even if you think your current options are limited or you are exhausted and feel that you can't possibly make any more effort with current projects. You may have to surrender to the knowledge that you are facing difficulties but, despite this, you must remain optimistic and believe that you will ultimately be successful.

48

CHING THE WELL

A town may change its location but it can never change the position of its well, which always provides the water that the people need. Trust that you will be abundant and prosperous in everything that you do and that your needs will always be satisfied. However, you must guard against being overly ambitious or too greedy because that will lead to problems for you.

49

KÖ REVOLUTION

If you want to make changes you must do so gradually in order to win everyone's support and not alienate them. You must also prove that what you are suggesting is needed and can work, otherwise you won't get the backing you desire. Show that you've got the intelligence to make things happen and at the right time, and then you'll be successful.

50

TING THE CAULDRON

This is a very auspicious hexagram because it promises great success if you behave in ways that will benefit other people. Traditionally, food was cooked in the cauldron before being offered to God. You therefore need to act in ways that will help and nourish other people, even if that involves making sacrifices yourself. Fate plays a part in this and you must accept its role in your life.

51

CHÊN SHOCK

Despite having to cope with momentous changes and upheavals which make you fearful or worried, everything will work out very well for you in the long run. There will be far fewer repercussions from these changes than you feared, especially if you behave cautiously and with moderation. Even though times are difficult, don't neglect the simple pleasures of life.

52

KÊN STILLNESS

True peace of mind and tranquillity come from being active when that is necessary and being still when that is what's required. When everything happens at its proper time you will make great progress. It's important to be mindful of everything that you are doing and to concentrate on it so you can give it all your focus. Don't let your mind drift toward other concerns.

53

CHIEN GRADUAL DEVELOPMENT

This is a period of slow and steady progress, and eventually you'll be successful. Everything must happen in its own time, so don't try to rush things or tackle them in the wrong order. Be patient and circumspect, and then everything will develop at its own pace. Take everything slowly and carefully but without allowing situations to stagnate or grind to a halt.

54

KUEI MEI THE MARRYING MAIDEN

This hexagram is named after the story of the young girl who gets married and doesn't behave in an appropriate manner. It warns you to be aware of the pitfalls and potential problems that lie in wait for you, and to avoid them whenever possible. This isn't a good time to force your hand or to manipulate a situation to your advantage because that will work out badly for you.

55

FÊNG ABUNDANCE

This is a very abundant and prosperous time for you, so enjoy it while it lasts. Share your prosperity with others instead of hoarding it. However, you must avoid fretting about what will happen if this abundance starts to diminish and your run of good fortune begins to change. Be like the Sun at noon when it's at its zenith, and shine the light of your prosperity on everyone around you.

56

LÜ THE WANDERER

You must be like a wanderer who is in strange lands and dependent on the kindness of strangers. Behave with propriety and humility, and don't waste your energy by getting caught up in activities that don't matter or by being too much on the move. It's a good time to make progress in minor matters rather than to become involved in anything very important.

57

SUN GENTLE EFFECTIVENESS

It's a time of gentle progress, when you make small steps rather than giant leaps. Don't try to browbeat people into agreeing with what you want. Instead, simply persevere and be content with tiny victories. These will be much more enduring and successful. It might help to ask the advice of someone you respect or who's in a position of authority over you.

58

TUI JOY

This is the hexagram of happiness and joyful satisfaction. You must persevere in whatever you do, and also behave correctly and with firmness. Keep joy in your heart and allow it to lighten your spirits, because concentrating on whatever makes you happy will brighten your life and keep you cheerful. Enjoy talking to your friends and taking part in activities with them.

HUAN DISPERSAL

You must be single-minded when doing things that are important to you or when moving ahead with projects. It's also a good time for travel. Don't allow your thoughts or your energies to become distracted because then you'll lose focus and might behave in ways that you'll later regret. A devout spiritual or religious practice will help you to concentrate on what's important.

CHIEH LIMITATION

Be firm with yourself and place any limitations on yourself that you think are necessary. However, you must know where to draw the line so that you don't become so strict with yourself that you make your life a misery. You must be equally careful when placing restrictions on others because they'll soon object if they think you are being too tough on them. Be moderate when imposing these limitations.

61

CHUNG FU INNER SINCERITY

Show that you are sincere in what you do and that you have faith in your convictions and beliefs. Rid yourself of any prejudice and be open to other people so you can truly understand them. It is important to be selfless whenever possible because this will help you to cope with even the most difficult situations. Travel is especially beneficial at this time.

62

HSIAO KUO SMALL SUCCESSES

This isn't a time when you should aim high or be too ambitious because you are unlikely to get very far. Instead, concentrate on small tasks and activities in which you stand a much greater chance of being successful. Make sure that you can tell the difference between what is really important and what is of little consequence, especially when deciding what to spend your money on.

63

CHI CHI COMPLETION AND THE NEXT STEP

You have achieved a great deal and should feel pleased with all your efforts. However, your work isn't over yet because there are still some loose ends that must be tied up before they start to unravel and create problems for you. Act quickly before this happens. You should also bear in mind that various circumstances, despite being orderly, could cause problems in the long term.

64

WEI CHI BEFORE COMPLETION

The change from chaos to order hasn't happened yet, even though you are doing everything possible to encourage it. Tread carefully and don't take unnecessary risks that could have a negative impact on everything that you've achieved so far. You should certainly guard against being complacent about your eventual success because that could definitely lead to problems and setbacks.

A SAMPLE I CHING READING

If you consult a book devoted to the I Ching you'll see that the process of casting each line of a hexagram is slightly more complicated than that given here.

In a full I Ching reading, some lines are called "moving lines." You draw the hexagram and interpret it in the usual way, but you then redraw the moving lines so that broken lines become solid and vice versa. You then read this new hexagram to expand on the meaning of the first. The procedure has had to be shortened in this book for reasons of space yet it still gives you a good I Ching reading.

POSING THE QUESTION

Kirsty wants to know whether she should remove her daughter, Janet, from the school she attends. Janet is unhappy at her school and Kirsty suspects that this is partly because she is being bullied. Kirsty's question is therefore "Please give me insight into whether Janet should change schools."

THE THROWS

The first throw added up to seven, giving a solid line. The second throw was six, giving a broken line. The third added up to eight, giving a broken line. The fourth added up to seven, which is a solid line. The fifth added up to eight, which is a broken line. The sixth added up to seven, which is a solid line. The upper trigram is *Li* and the lower one is *Chên*, and when combined they form the 21st hexagram, which is *Shih Ho* or Biting Through.

THE HEXAGRAM

Shih Ho told Kirsty that she needed to take firm action to sort out her daughter's problems at school. The interpretation mentions taking legal action if necessary, but Kirsty thought this was going too far. Instead, she decided to talk to the teachers at Janet's school about the bullying while encouraging Janet to stand up for herself, but without becoming a bully in the process. She would work through these processes first before looking for another school for Janet.

When you write down the hexagram, make sure that you always start from the bottom.

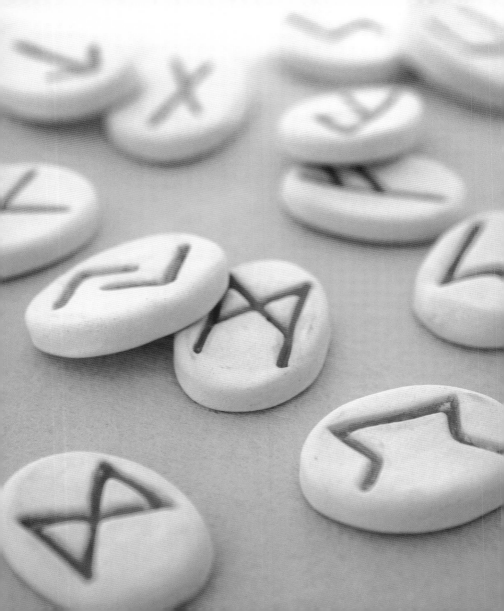

PART NINE

Runes

HOW RUNES WORK

Runes have a strong flavor of the mysterious. They are one of the most evocative divination techniques because they carry profound echoes of the past and of the ancient Viking lands from which they came.

Even the story of how runes were developed is strange—legend has it that Odin, the Norse god, suspended himself upside down from *Yggdrasil*, the Tree of Life, in order to attain enlightenment. After hanging there for nine days and nights, he saw the runes lying at his feet.

Runes continue to have an otherworldly quality, of being out of step with our 21st-century existence, and as such they have something very valuable to offer us.

You can buy a variety of sets of runes, although the most popular contains 24 runes and is known as the Elder Futhark. Some sets now contain 25 because they include a blank rune as well. You can make your own runes or you can buy ready-made sets. As with any other divination technique, it's important to choose a set that you like. You can either keep the runes in the box or bag in which they came or make your own. What is important is to treat

them with respect and to keep them in a safe place when they are not being used.

NON-INVERTIBLE AND INVERTIBLE RUNES

When you study the runes you'll notice that some look the same whichever way up you hold them. These are called non-invertible runes. With others, there is an obvious difference, and these are the invertible runes. Invertible runes have two meanings, according to whether they are upright or reversed when you draw them.

CASTING THE RUNES

One of the best ways to cast the runes is to draw a single rune in answer to a question. For instance, you could say "Please give me insight into my domestic life" and then

Odin, the Norse god, is said to have seen runes at his feet.

Keep your runes in a special bag or box when they're not in use.

select a rune to give you the answer. You can keep your runes in a bag and rummage through them until you feel compelled to choose one, or you can lay them out on a flat surface, face down, and pick one. Choosing a single rune pinpoints the precise issues that need your attention at that moment. Sometimes, the runes will ignore your question and talk about something completely different, in which case you must be open to their message. They are telling you that you must switch your focus to some other area of your life and you will undoubtedly know what this is, especially if you are avoiding it.

YES OR NO?

Another option is to ask a question to which there is a yes or no response. Again, you draw a single rune. If it's upright, the answer is "yes." If it's reversed, the answer is "no." If it's a non-invertible rune, you must draw another. And if you draw Wyrd, the blank rune (assuming you're using a set of 25 runes), it's not the right time to ask the question. This might be because, unbeknownst to you, the situation has already resolved itself.

MULTIPLE RUNE READINGS

There are times when you need to examine a situation in detail. For instance, you might want to look at three different areas of your life, such as your home, health, and work, or you might want insight into your past, present, and future. Cast one rune for each category and then interpret them accordingly.

Alternatively, you can follow an ancient tradition by scattering the runes from the bag and paying attention to those that fall face-up. Experiment until you find the method that suits you best, or simply follow whichever method seems appropriate at the time.

Whichever method of rune-casting you opt for, always open yourself to the inherent mystery of the runes and to their accuracy and pertinence. On the following pages are in-depth interpretations of each of the 24 runes of the Elder Futhark. Ponder their meanings and let them work on your imagination to get the most out of them.

Try scattering the runes from the bag and seeing which fall face-up.

FEHU

*Fehu's traditional meaning is linked with cattle,
which can be bred for money and eaten for food.*

Fehu's two contemporary meanings are food
and money. However, you must consider
both these meanings in their widest
context. Food, when related to Fehu, means
nourishment on all levels. It might be the
food you eat but it could also be spiritual
replenishment, emotional sustenance, or the
nourishment that comes from using your
creative talents.

Fehu therefore asks you what you most
value in life, and whether this receives the
attention it deserves. Is it money, is it family
life, or something else that feeds you? It
also tells you to take care of your
possessions and to fully appreciate them.

INVERTED

When Fehu is inverted,
it speaks of frustration
and difficulties. It also
warns of losing something
that you value.

URUZ

Many centuries ago, this rune was connected with the wild oxen known as aurochs.

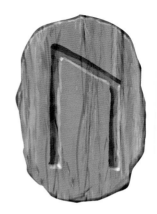

Uruz is associated with strength, because not only were the aurochs strong but it took considerable strength for humans to control them. Therefore there is a very solid and grounded quality to this rune. It describes strength of character and strength of will, in addition to physical stamina. Oxen were beasts of burden, so sometimes Uruz describes having to bear a heavy load with courage and fortitude.

Another meaning of Uruz is the need to be responsible for your actions and not to lose control of your wilder nature. For instance, you might have to rein in your anger or aggression, and know when to hold back and when to push forward.

Oxen are traditionally connected with the rune Uruz.

INVERTED

When Uruz is inverted, it has two meanings. It can mean losing your strength and energy, whether physically or mentally, or it can describe allowing your behavior to become out of control.

THURISAZ

This is a challenging rune because it's linked with upheavals, chaos and aggression. Life doesn't go according to plan when Thurisaz is in evidence.

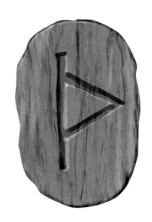

Traditionally, Thurisaz is linked with Thor, the god of thunder, and therefore you may be facing some form of cataclysm in your life. It may feel as though you are losing contact with the ground beneath your feet and you don't know what's going to happen next. Sometimes, trouble can strike like a bolt from the blue.

However, although this rune speaks of disruptive and discordant situations, it does reassure you that all this chaos is happening for a reason. It is intended to teach you valuable lessons about your life and will lead on to a more positive and sustainable time.

INVERTED
When Thurisaz is inverted, its negative qualities are greatly reduced and the situation is not nearly so dire or difficult.

ANSUZ

Sometimes called "the god rune," Ansuz has close links with the protection that Odin gives his followers.

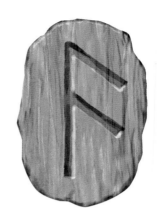

Odin handed down a great deal of wisdom to his devotees, and Ansuz rules every form of communication. This can be personal or technological, formal or informal, in books or the spoken word.

Ansuz is also connected to ancestors and therefore to people we respect. The rune is telling us that we can learn a great deal from these people, either through their experiences or when they give us direct information. So if you're in need of advice, Ansuz is telling you to talk to someone you respect and admire. Equally, it indicates that you may soon be in a position of authority yourself, and able to share your wisdom and insight with others.

INVERTED

When Ansuz is inverted it speaks of difficulties in communicating with others, whether because information has become scrambled or there is an age gap between the people concerned.

Thor was the mighty god of thunder.

RAIDO

This is the rune of journeys, whether they're physical, mental, emotional, or spiritual. Journeys come in many forms, which is something you need to remember when interpreting Raido.

Raido rules all types of journeys: emotional and physical, and even the fact that life itself is a huge journey that is often taken without many signposts along the way. To take this analogy further, Raido refers to movement and action, so can represent modes of transport such as a car.

Raido also describes the need to move forward in our lives, especially at times when we've become stuck and prefer to cling to what is familiar. It may be that we need to take action or be the instigator of a new project or venture.

The resin in pine trees is highly inflammable, so the Vikings used its branches for torches.

INVERTED

When inverted, Raido describes a period in which plans don't work out in the way you were expecting. Journeys may be disrupted or canceled, too.

KAUNAZ

This rune is connected with fire. Originally, it was linked with the pine trees from which Vikings made torches, so it can describe the need to shed light on your life in order to see the way ahead.

Kaunaz also describes fiery enthusiasm for a new enterprise, the light of knowledge, or the sudden illumination that comes when you have an important realization. It's linked to knowledge and understanding, and also with promise and success.

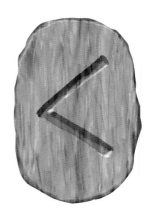

Kaunaz can also refer to the white heat of sexual passion, the warmth that comes from a solid friendship, or the initial spark that draws you to another person. But no matter what it describes, Kaunaz warns us not to let its fire burn out of control or to fizzle out through neglect.

INVERTED

When Kaunaz is inverted, it speaks of the loss of a friendship or some other relationship. Perhaps it has burnt itself out. It also warns of the perils of ignorance and, conversely, of being too clever for your own good.

GEBO

One of the most beneficial and positive runes,
Gebo means gifts, generosity, and partnerships.

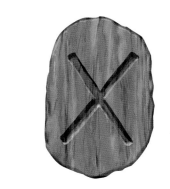

Gebo is the symbol for a kiss, so it's no
surprise that this is one of the runes linked
with love in all its forms. This could be
platonic, passionate, or the love that a
parent has for his child. Love can bring
great happiness but sometimes it can lead
to problems, so Gebo may be warning
about difficulties in a relationship,
especially if someone is feeling very needy.

Gebo represents gifts, which may be
simple presents from one person to another
or might be the talents and skills that the
Vikings believed were conferred on us by
the gods. This rune may therefore be
telling you to make greater use of your
own gifts, whatever these may be. They
will bring you happiness and emotional
satisfaction. Gebo can also describe
working for a higher purpose that benefits
all of humanity, such as charity work. Gebo
is a non-invertible rune.

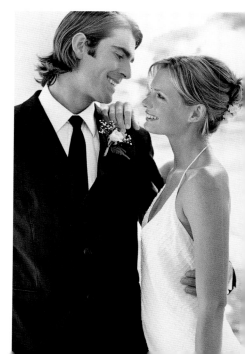

WUNJO

Wunjo is a lovely rune because it describes happiness, contentment, and harmony.

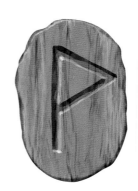

Wunjo can describe the joy that comes from a balanced and harmonious relationship between two people, such as a stable marriage or a long-term friendship.It also speaks of the benefits of being content with your lot, rather than wishing for things that will never happen.

If you are single when you draw this rune, it may be telling you that a new and happy relationship is on the way. Wunjo is also a favorable rune for any sort of business partnership that's getting off the ground because again it promises that this will go well. Your social life may become very busy when this rune appears, and it will bring you enjoyment.

INVERTED

When inverted, Wunjo describes wishes and hopes that fail to materialize. It can also refer to a relationship that goes through a testing time, or a sense of being isolated from the people around you. It also speaks of the benefits of being content with your lot, rather than wishing for things that will never happen.

Wunjo is one of the most positive runes and is associated with happy relationships.

HAGALAZ

This is a very challenging rune because it describes situations that are out of your control, in which you feel you are being swept along by something larger than yourself.

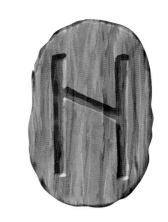

Hagalaz is traditionally connected to hail and to other destructive natural forces. All we can do in such conditions is to take shelter and wait for the storm to pass. Hagalaz may therefore be telling you to surrender to the inevitable, however that may present itself in your life, and to accept that there's nothing you can do about it yourself. This is a time of great learning for you, when you can be strong in the face of difficulties rather than collapse in a heap.

Hagalaz is a reminder to draw on your moral courage and grit while the difficult situation lasts. The position will eventually change for the better but in the meantime you must accept that you are powerless to alter it: the matter is out of your hands. Hagalaz is a non-invertible rune.

Hagalaz refers to situations that are worrying and which present us with challenges.

NAUTHIZ

This rune means "need," and is therefore often linked to crises. You might need more money, a bigger home, a job, some medical help, or someone who will love you.

Whatever it is that you're longing for, Nauthiz is telling you to work hard to get it. But first you must decide exactly what it is that you want, so you can concentrate on it and therefore stand a good chance of attracting it. You must be prepared to look at the situation from a new angle in case you've overlooked an obvious solution to the problem. In addition, you may have to think on your feet and be inventive, so don't let your ideas become stuck in a rut.

Nauthiz can also represent friction—either created by a challenging situation that spurs you into taking action or the difficulties caused when two people rub each other up the wrong way. You need to find a way to resolve it without resorting to blaming others or dissolving into nervous anxiety. Nauthiz is a non-invertible rune.

Nauthiz signifies a crisis or friction between two people in personal or work life.

ISA

Isa has the uncompromising meaning of "ice." Ice reveals the essence of Isa: something is being held in a frozen or inanimate state.

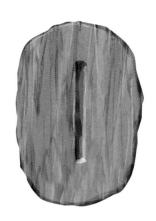

A situation may have become blocked and you can't move forward: it may be stagnant emotions caused by a resistance to inevitable change, or a time when you feel you've gone into hibernation. Very often, Isa describes a reluctance to let your life develop in the way it should, coupled with a longing to cling on to the status quo even though it no longer serves you in the way that it once did.

Isa can indicate a time when it seems impossible for you to proceed with your plans, even though you want to do so. They hit delays or deadlocks, and your only option is to wait patiently for these difficulties to pass. Isa can also describe a time of rest and recuperation after tremendous effort or ill health, when you have to retreat into yourself. Isa is a non-invertible rune.

Isa is the rune that's associated with ice.

JERA

Jera is connected with the cycles of nature, with the seasonal round, and the turning point of the year that comes with the winter solstice.

Jera is linked with time and the experience and wisdom that we can only accumulate over time. It can describe the gentle changes that take place in life and which

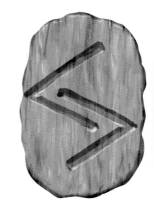

are almost imperceptible, but which, in hindsight, seem so clear and obvious.

Jera is also linked with harvest, another major turning point of the year. It usually refers to harvesting the results of your previous actions, which is karma by another name. Karmic law states that you always reap what you sow, even though it may come back to you in a form that you weren't expecting. So Jera is telling you to behave carefully if you don't want to have to deal with the results of your actions. Not all karma is unfortunate, of course, so Jera may be promising you that you will soon reap the rich harvest of previous hard work or kindness. Jera is a non-invertible rune.

EIHWAZ

This is a mysterious rune because it's connected with the secrets that surround life and death.

Traditionally, Eihwaz is linked with Yggdrasil, the tree from which Odin hung in his quest for enlightenment. This was a time of great endurance for him, and therefore Eihwaz encourages us to be strong and firm when faced by the trials and tribulations of life. It teaches that we encounter these difficulties for a reason, and that facing them head-on makes us stronger and more resilient. Such challenges aren't easy lessons to learn, nor are they meant to be. They are intended to test us and to help us grow as a result.

Its association with death means that Eihwaz can also describe an inheritance. This might be money passed from one generation to the next, or a gift or talent handed down. Sometimes, it can indicate an inherited illness that will test the endurance and patience of everyone who is involved. Eihwaz is a non-invertible rune.

Eihwaz is the rune that's primarily associated with Yggdrasil, the Tree of Life.

PERTH

All of the runes have a rather strange quality but Perth is by far the most mysterious.

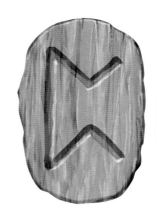

Perth is strongly linked with *wyrd*, or fate, and may therefore appear in readings when you feel as though you're caught in the grip of something numinous and ineffable. Perth tells you to go beyond the superficialities in order to delve deeply into what's really going on. Avoid trite or easy assumptions and be prepared to analyze the situation from every angle, and also to put your own behavior and motivations under the microscope. Yet throughout all this you must remain open to the idea of unseen forces guiding you.

Perth has connections with the mystery of life, and is therefore linked to all forms of creativity. This might be the birth of a child or the development of an artistic venture, especially if it has spiritual overtones or it seems to be tapping into the realm of the collective unconscious. Perhaps you don't understand how such an idea could have come to you.

INVERTED

When it's inverted, Perth refers to fears that may be blown out of proportion.

ALGIZ

This is the rune of protection and it can also be used to invoke the gods.

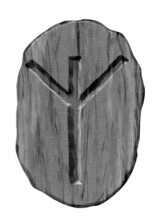

Algiz is the perfect rune to select as a talisman or *sigil* if you want to practice your psychic powers or spend a lot of time meditating. It also offers very strong protection if you want to give healing to someone. Algiz urges you to take better care of yourself in other areas of your life as well, whether that means protecting your health by eating sensibly or by being more careful about the company you keep in case you mix with people who will harm you in some way.

Algiz also describes people to whom you look up and who act as mentors or parental figures. It might represent a beloved teacher or spiritual guide. In addition, it can signify a vocation or spiritual quest.

INVERTED

When inverted, Algiz describes being on the defensive and primed for attack. It can also signify being used.

SOWELU

This is the rune of the Sun, without which there would be no life on our planet nor in our solar system.

Sowelu refers to the solar principles of life-giving power, vitality, confidence, and optimism. As a result, when it appears in a reading it can confer all these qualities and encourage you to make the best of yourself or to push ahead with a particular project. It also describes wholeness and completion.

Sowelu encourages you to keep going even when times are tough, and to believe that they'll soon improve. In the meantime, you can draw on your own strength of purpose and practice the art of positive thinking. It is a good rune to draw if you've been ill because it promises that your health will soon improve. It is a very positive rune and will always help to balance any of the more difficult runes when they appear together in a reading. It is a good rune to use as a talisman or form of protection if you want to practice healing. Sowelu is a non-invertible rune.

The solar principle of Sowelu urges us to keep going when life is difficult.

TEIWAZ

Teiwaz looks like an arrow pointing upward when it's in its upright position, which is a clue to its meaning.

Teiwaz indicates strength of purpose, courage, determination, and the ability to persevere, in the face of difficulty. It tells you to gather your resources, prepare for battle and stand up for what you think is right. Traditionally, Viking warriors would go into battle wearing bracelets inscribed with this rune, so it has powerful links with life-and-death struggles.

Not every struggle has to feel like a fight to the death, but Teiwaz always has a competitive flavor so it's a good rune to draw if you're planning to take part in a sporting activity. It's also favorable for business matters in which you want to beat the competition.

Berkana is linked with the birch tree.

INVERTED

When inverted, Teiwaz describes a loss of direction and focus, as well as some form of defeat or loss.

BERKANA

This rune has powerful links with fertility, motherhood and nurturing in general.

Berkana is strongly connected with all forms of birth, whether the literal birth of a child, the metaphorical birth of an idea, or the creative birth of an artistic enterprise. It's a life-giving rune and is especially effective when worn as a protective talisman. Its nurturing aspect tells you to take great care of anything that has just

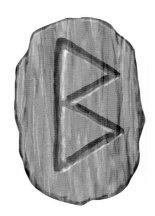

sprouted into life, whether this is a baby, a plant, or a project. Look after it and don't let it die through lack of attention.

Berkana is also linked with the birch tree, and may therefore suggest that you need to spend more time surrounded by nature. Its associations with fertility may be encouraging you to cultivate plants. It can also describe something that is still hidden from the world, such as a secret.

INVERTED

When inverted, Berkana denotes an inability to grow and develop.

EHWAZ

This rune is connected with horses, who once helped humans to travel, so Ehwaz is the rune of travel.

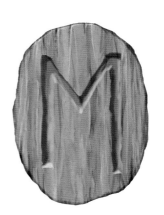

Ehwaz is linked to any form of physical travel, whether it's a short journey, a vacation, emigration, or change of location.

Working horses need to establish a harmonious relationship with their human riders and Ehwaz can therefore refer to an effective partnership in which both parties have a great deal to contribute. Horses are social animals and dislike being on their own, so this rune can describe the pleasure that comes from having people in your life whom you like and trust, or with whom you can work. It also describes working in tandem with others, being co-operative and having the flexibility to adapt to other people's personalities.

INVERTED

When inverted, Ehwaz describes an inflexible attitude, indecisiveness, and a betrayal of your trust.

Horses used to help farmers to work their land, creating the partnership which Ehwaz describes.

MANNAZ

Mannaz is connected to mankind, and especially refers to our ability to think rationally and to use our intelligence.

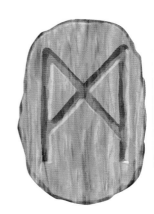

It encourages open-mindedness and objectivity. If you are using the runes to tell your fortune, Mannaz refers to the people in your life. You will learn about their attitude toward you and the way they influence you from the other runes that appear in the reading.

If you are struggling with a difficult relationship, Mannaz suggests that you should examine all your relationships with an objective eye to see if you are repeating unhelpful patterns. Have you fallen into a trap to which you've been blind until now? It is also a very encouraging rune if you are considering embarking on a spiritual quest, you want to improve your education, or you'll soon be embroiled in a legal matter. Even so, you should be aware of your behavior.

INVERTED

When inverted, Mannaz refers to a closed and prejudiced mind.

LAGUZ

This rune is connected with water, and therefore has symbolic links with the unconscious as the two are so strongly connected.

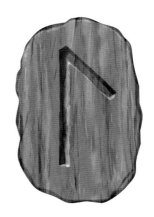

Laguz is an encouraging rune to draw if you are hoping to develop your psychic powers because it describes going deep into the unconscious and connecting with the occult. It is telling you to detach yourself from your conscious, critical mind and to let your impressions flow without judging them. This rune may also be telling you to pay more attention to your dreams, interpreting them so they give you guidance and reveal information that you may not have noticed in your waking life.

Water is the great cleanser, so sometimes Laguz is telling you to cleanse your life of someone or something that no longer belongs in it. Alternatively, you might need to cleanse yourself of some emotional baggage that's holding you back.

INVERTED

When inverted, Laguz describes fear, emotional blackmail, and lack of courage, whether it's mental or physical.

INGUZ

Inguz is connected with Frey, the ancient Scandinavian god of fertility. It is therefore one of the runes associated with fertility.

Inguz has a more male aspect than the other runes. It has strong connections with agriculture, and therefore can describe the need to become more attuned to nature by growing crops or tending your own garden. It refers to the seed stage of a project, when the initial idea has germinated and it now needs the right conditions in which to grow. This might be a plant but it could equally be a creative project, a fetus in a mother's womb or anything else that is springing into life. It can even refer to a relationship that is just getting off the ground. Whatever has germinated needs to be carefully nurtured and encouraged.

Inguz also encourages us to be thankful for what we've been given, even when times are difficult and we struggle to carry on. Inguz is a non-invertible rune.

Frey, the god of fertility, has close links with Inguz, which is the rune of growth.

OTHILA

This is the rune of inheritance and of the home, so it often refers to land or possessions that are passed down from one generation to the next.

Such valuable assets can be a source of great pleasure and wealth, or they can generate discord. Othila can also describe the genetic inheritance passed down through the generations and also the beliefs and behavior that children learn from their parents. Sometimes, this rune tells you to discover your true self amid all the conditioning that you've received.

Othila is a favorable rune to draw if you are considering a house move because it suggests that this will have a happy outcome. It is also a good time to become involved in legal affairs relating to property.

INVERTED

When inverted, Othila can describe holding on to a past way of life and refusing to accept any form of change. It can also indicate racism and greed.

DAGAZ

Dagaz is the rune of day and is linked with the summer solstice, when we have the maximum amount of daylight.

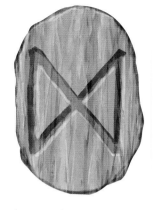

This is the final rune of the Elder Futhark and therefore represents the completion of one cycle and the beginning of another. Dagaz is the companion rune to Jera, which rules the winter solstice. The summer solstice is a turning point in the Sun's journey through the sky and Dagaz is therefore associated with change and new beginnings. These can sometimes be quite radical and dramatic. Despite this, Dagaz usually signifies beneficial and positive changes.

Through its connections with light and the summer solstice, which marks the longest day of the year, Dagaz is linked with enlightenment. This can be on a mental, emotional, or spiritual level but, whatever its nature, it will have a transforming and transcendent impact on your life. Dagaz can also describe the welcome light that comes after a period of darkness, such as going through a depressive phase and finally feeling that this is melting away and being replaced by greater contentment and peace. It's as though the sun is shining on you again. Another meaning of Dagaz is the breakthrough that comes after a period of stagnation and stalemate, when things are moving again at last. Dagaz is a non-invertible rune.

Othila can refer to the possessions that we inherit from our relatives.

SAMPLE RUNE READING

As there are several different ways to cast runes, it is a good idea to choose the method that is either the most suitable way to answer your question or which feels most appropriate to you at the time. You can be quite flexible about this, so allow your intuition to guide you.

JON'S QUESTIONS

Jon wanted guidance about the state of his life, and especially about his home life, his career, and his relationship with his father. He was considering changing his career and moving to another part of the country, but was worried about how this would affect his elderly father as he would no longer be living near him. As this was clearly a reading of three categories—his home, his career, and his relationships—Jon drew three runes from the bag. The set of runes being used was the 25-rune set, which includes the blank rune known as Wyrd.

HOME LIFE

The rune describing Jon's home life was Wyrd. This rune speaks of radical change, of

Always treat the runes with respect when you're working with them.

total transformation from one stage of life to another. In Jon's case, it described his decision to move to a completely different part of the country, with all the upheaval that this would entail. Wyrd, in its association with dramatic change, encouraged this move.

CAREER

Dagaz was the rune selected for Jon's career. Another rune of radical change, it perfectly described his decision to completely alter his career and start again. When asked why he was considering such a dramatic change in his life, Jon admitted that his current job made him feel depressed and despondent. Dagaz is connected with breakthroughs and a lightening of the spirit.

RELATIONSHIPS

The third rune, to represent Jon's relationship with his father, was Wunjo. This speaks of the companionship that comes from being with kindred spirits and the ability to accept the circumstances in which we find ourselves. It therefore reassured Jon that his father would be happy for his son to move away and that he would find other companions to prevent him becoming lonely.

Laying the runes out on a black cloth helps to create a ritual for reading them.

PART TEN

Face reading

HOW FACE READING WORKS

There is an old saying that your face is your fortune. And many facereaders would agree, because your face speaks volumes about your character. This will inevitably influence the path you take through life and, therefore, the events that happen to you along the way.

FACT OR OLD WIVES' TALES?

Most of us already interpret character by looking at the faces of those we meet, even if we aren't aware of it. Someone whose eyes are too close together is often thought of as shifty, a bulbous nose is said to indicate a heavy drinker, and pinched lips are believed to indicate a mean nature. When you look at someone with any of these characteristics you may not even be conscious that you are registering such thoughts, but nevertheless you'll already have formed a strong opinion about this person. The question we need to examine here is whether these are ideas backed up by convincing evidence.

FACE READING AROUND THE WORLD

Many cultures practice face reading. It's a very popular form of divination in China, and the art of Chinese face reading has now spread to the West. However, face reading was already practiced in Europe—the Victorians particularly enjoyed physiognomy (reading the face) and phrenology (reading the bumps on the head).

PRACTICING FACE READING

If you are new to face reading, it will be easiest to begin with your own face. Draw your hair back off your face so you can see the shape of your head and face clearly. Stand or sit directly in front of a mirror, with a good source of natural light that doesn't throw misleading shadows across your face. Do your best to be objective by analyzing each feature first, such as the size of your eyes, and then looking up its meaning. This will prevent you altering the facts to fit the meaning that you prefer.

It's always easiest to begin face reading by working with your own face. But you must do your best to be objective about what you see!

FACE SHAPES

As with any other form of divination it pays to be systematic, so start by analyzing the shape of your face or that of someone else. The Chinese divide the face into five shapes and name them according to the five Chinese elements. In reality, it's quite rare to find someone with a face that belongs to only one element; most of our faces are a mixture of at least two different elements.

THE METAL FACE

This is an oval face with wide cheekbones, clear eyes, pale eyebrows, straight hair, and a pale complexion. The person is usually good-looking, with a lively sense of humor. Sensitive and creative, this person has a delicate nervous system and should be careful about what she eats.

THE WOOD FACE

A Wood face is long and narrow with a broad, wide forehead. The hair and eyebrows are fine. A Wood type likes to make plans and always needs new directions in which to grow, becoming angry and frustrated if she feels the way ahead is blocked. She should avoid foods that compromise her liver.

THE EARTH FACE

An Earth face is square and short with a strong jaw-line and a large mouth. The person probably has a stocky body and a deep voice. An Earth type is practical, resourceful, and reliable, with a tendency to follow tradition that can make her quite stubborn and resistant to change.

THE WATER FACE

Someone with a Water face has a soft, round face with large, liquid eyes and dark hair. She often has a chubby body. This person is quiet, sensitive, and highly tuned to her emotions. Friends find her sympathetic and easy to talk to. She is ambitious but at times she can struggle to motivate herself.

THE FIRE FACE

Someone with a Fire face has a long, narrow face with a pointed chin and a narrow forehead. Unlike the Wood type, the hair and eyebrows are thick and wiry. The bodily movements are quick, and the person is infectiously enthusiastic about life. She enjoys taking risks and living life to the full.

OTHER CONSIDERATIONS

After you've analyzed the shape of someone's face according to the element that it belongs to, there are other considerations that you need to take into account.

THE CROWN OF THE HEAD

This part of the head will tell you whether someone is confident or insecure. Essentially, the higher the crown, the more confidence and ambition a person has. Therefore, someone with a very high crown can be quite bossy and authoritarian, behaving as though she really is wearing a crown. Equally, someone with a very low crown feels insecure and inferior.

HAIR

Hair is considered very important in Chinese face reading. The texture, color, quality, and profusion of someone's hair gives many clues about her character.

Fine hair This indicates someone who is sensitive and may be physically fragile, especially if she is slender.

Thick, wiry hair This indicates someone who has robust health and physical prowess. She has good powers of recuperation when ill and enjoys rising to challenges.

Long, curly hair shows someone who likes to be active and independent.

A shaved head is an indication of tremendous reserves of energy.

Curly hair Someone with naturally curly hair is active and energetic. If a person feels the need to curl her hair, perhaps with a perm, it shows that she needs to introduce more energy into her life.

Straight hair Someone with naturally straight hair is easy-going and a relaxing companion. Someone who makes a point of straightening her hair wants to cultivate these qualities within herself.

Long hair The person with long hair is considerate and practical. She's a free thinker and needs to go her own way through life.

Short hair The shorter the hair, the more decisive the person. Very short, cropped hair indicates someone who is ambitious, dynamic, and possibly aggressive.

Shaved hair Someone with a shaved head is full of dynamic energy, which can make her restless, aggressive, short-tempered, and tense.

THE EYES

The eyes are said to be the windows of the soul, so they are very instructive about someone's character. When analyzing someone's face, don't forget that the person may be wearing make-up that's designed to accentuate the eyes. This may change the apparent shape of the eyes, so do try to look beyond this.

Eyes that are set far apart belong to someone who is versatile and flexible.

LARGE EYES

Someone with naturally large eyes has an open, friendly nature. He likes to view life from a wide perspective and enjoys plenty of variety in his life. He certainly doesn't like to be tied down by trivial details and petty restrictions.

SMALL EYES

When someone has small eyes, he is skilled at concentrating on details. He tends to view life from a narrow perspective, so he excels at being a specialist, researcher, or expert. He finds it difficult to open up emotionally to strangers so it can take a while to get to know him well.

WIDELY SPACED EYES

Someone with widely spaced eyes is broad-minded and versatile. He enjoys discussing a tremendous variety of topics because he's interested in so many different issues and ideas. Routine is anathema to him.

CLOSELY SPACED EYES

The person whose eyes are closely spaced, so there's very little gap between the inner corner of his eyes and the bridge of his nose, likes to look at life in great detail. This gives him great powers of concentration but can also lead to obsessive and narrow-minded tendencies. He enjoys following a structured routine.

DEEP-SET EYES

The person with deep-set eyes is very private and reluctant to reveal too much of his personality to others. He likes to play his cards close to his chest, which can make him seem secretive and emotionally withdrawn.

Small eyes reveal an ability to concentrate on details and facts.

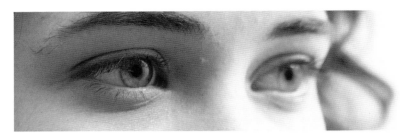

Large irises signify an emotional but kind character.

PROTRUDING EYES

When someone's eyes appear to bulge outward, he is enthusiastic and curious about the world. He is very versatile and is easily bored, so can find it difficult to follow one activity for long.

UPWARD-SLANTING EYES

When the outer corners of the eyes slant upward, like those of a cat, the person is an optimist. He knows what he wants from life and he's not afraid to ask for it.

DOWNWARD-SLANTING EYES

When the outer corners of the eye slant downward, the person finds it hard to stand up to other people. He may also have pessimistic tendencies.

UNEVENLY SET EYES

When someone's eyes aren't level, so one is higher than the other, it shows that he has an unusual and possibly unorthodox way of viewing the world. He has tremendous insight and is able to analyze situations from a unique perspective.

IRISES

Pay attention to the size and position of the iris within the eye. A large iris, so that very little white of the eye is visible, indicates someone who's very emotional, demonstrative, and kind. If the white of the eye is visible above the iris, the person has a powerful temper and should therefore be handled carefully by those around them. If the white of the eye is visible below the iris, the person is hard to please and has difficulties in coping with life.

EYEBROWS

Don't forget to look at the person's eyebrows as well. These frame the face and give it structure. Some people, both male and female, like to pluck their eyebrows so you must take this into account. The stronger and longer the eyebrows, the more strength and vitality a person has. He's dynamic, energetic, and ambitious, with a vibrant and powerful personality. Conversely, someone with naturally sparse, thin or short eyebrows makes less of an impression on the world and may also be less physically robust.

When the outer corners of the eyes slant downward, their owner may be pessimistic.

THE NOSE

In Chinese face reading, the nose indicates a person's ability to attract money, as well as revealing something of her general character and emotional make-up.

PROMINENT NOSE

Someone whose face is dominated by her nose is driven by a particular interest or desire. Her life may be an emotional roller-coaster.

SMALL NOSE

The person with a small nose is good at controlling her emotions, so can give the impression of being shy and withdrawn. She likes to keep a tight grip on her finances.

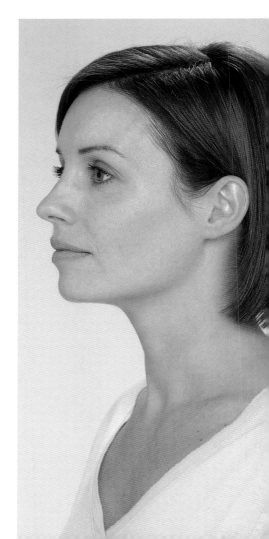

The fleshy tip of this woman's nose indicates a warm and gregarious personality.

LONG NOSE

Someone with a long and narrow nose likes to concentrate on a few topics at any one time, rather than to get emotionally involved in too many things at once.

WIDE NOSE

When someone has a wide, flat nose, she has many wide-ranging interests. She's very popular and sociable. However, it can be difficult for her to make decisions because she has so many options at her disposal.

BULBOUS NOSE

A bulbous end to a nose indicates a person who is ruled by her emotions and who reaches decisions based entirely on her emotional instincts. Someone whose nose ends in an exaggeratedly bulbous fashion may have a violent temper.

HARD-TIPPED NOSE

Someone whose nose ends in a pinched tip makes a habit of concentrating on the rational and objective side of life, and ignoring her emotional reactions.

A man with wide nostrils is likely be independent and self-sufficient.

INDENTED NOSE

If the tip of the person's nose is indented, it shows that she will go through a lot of emotional ups and downs in her life.

NOSTRILS

Pay close attention to a person's nostrils. Ideally, the nostrils should be somewhat hidden when you look at her, as this will ensure her financial success. Someone with wide, flaring nostrils is interested in many different aspects of life and enjoys taking on more than one task at once. She is independent and self-sufficient. Someone with narrow, small nostrils likes to specialize in one thing at a time. She depends on other people for support and encouragement.

THE MOUTH

The size and shape of our mouths reveals many secrets about us, including our emotions and sensuality.

WIDE MOUTH

Someone with a wide mouth is generous and friendly. He enjoys variety because he needs many different experiences in his life.

NARROW MOUTH

Someone with a narrow mouth, the edges of which are barely wider than the end of his nose, is very self-contained and has a need for independence.

FULL LIPS

The person with full lips is sensual and pleasure-loving. He needs plenty of enjoyment in his life.

THIN LIPS

When someone has thin lips it means he is emotionally withdrawn. He takes life seriously and can be very careful with his money. If the lips are also tightly pursed, the person is rather self-centered.

A very wide mouth shows innate generosity of spirit and emotional warmth.

DOWNWARD CURVING MOUTH

When someone's mouth curves downward, it shows a sense of discontent and dissatisfaction.

UPWARD CURVING MOUTH

This shows someone who is optimistic, friendly, and easy-going.

THE EARS

In Chinese face reading, the ears indicate wisdom as well as providing a glimpse of the person's general health.

PROTRUDING EARS

Prominent ears that stick out from the head indicate that the person has strong opinions and isn't afraid to talk about them.

SET CLOSE TO HEAD

When someone's ears are set close to his head, he is cautious and thrifty. He is concerned about what other people might think of him.

LARGE AND FLESHY EARS

The person with large ears is full of vitality. He is intelligent and lively.

SMALL EARS

When someone has small ears it shows that he relies on his instincts when making decisions. He may be very health-conscious.

FLESHY LOBES

Fleshy ear lobes show an independent streak. The person is reliable, resourceful and motivated.

SMALL OR NON-EXISTENT LOBES

These indicate someone who finds it hard to put his ideas into practice. He is easily deterred when projects fail to go well and may even give up on them.

Nicely shaped ears indicate good health and a strong constitution.

MOLES

One of the classic ways of telling your fortune is to do so from any moles that you have on your body.

ON THE FOREHEAD OR TEMPLE

A mole on the right indicates that money and success will arrive by chance. A mole on the left shows that the person's fortunes will fluctuate.

ON EITHER EYEBROW

This is a very fortunate marking because it shows a happy committed relationship and a happy domestic life.

BETWEEN THE EYEBROWS

A mole here indicates a fiery temper.

ON THE NOSE

If on the right side, the person enjoys traveling and needs many changes of scene. If on the left side, the person is changeable and can be unreliable.

ON THE CHEEK

If on the right side, it's a sign of a successful life. On the left side, success will be less easy to come by. On both cheeks, success will only come after a lot of effort.

ON THE LIP

This indicates a sensual nature.

ON THE CHIN

This is a very good place for a mole. It indicates that the person's fortune will increase as she gets older. She has artistic ability and strong common sense.

ON THE EAR

A mole found here suggests there will be problems connected with jealousy and gossip.

ON THE NECK

This is always a sign of success. Artistic abilities are shown by a mole on the front of the neck. Unexpected windfalls are shown by a mole on the side of the neck.

ON THE BREASTS

On the left breast, relationships will be of fundamental importance. On the right breast, the person will marry for business or financial reasons.

OVER THE HEART

The person is kind, loving and considerate.

ON THE ARMS

On the right arm, problems in early life will give way to contentment and success. On the left arm, business success.

ON THE STOMACH

Greed will eventually lead to bad luck.

ON EITHER HIP

A happy family life.

ON THE LEGS

On the right leg, the person is energetic. On the left leg, the person is lazy.

A mole on the upper lip indicates sensuality and a love of all the good things in life.

PART ELEVEN

Scrying

HOW SCRYING WORKS

The art of scrying is ancient. It involves gazing at a shiny surface, such as that of a crystal ball, and seeing images in it. These enable you to tell the future or gain insight into a situation that is troubling you. Scrying is thought to be thousands of years old, making it one of the oldest forms of divination.

The most common form of scrying uses a crystal ball, but you could easily use one of the ancient scrying techniques, such as gazing into a bowl of water or a mirror. Ideally, you should experiment to see which technique suits you best and with which you're most comfortable.

WHAT DO YOU SEE?

When you practice scrying, you may be lucky enough to see visions unfolding before you in precise detail, rather as though you are watching a film. However, your psychic abilities may not take this form at all, in which case you will have to trust your intuition. Rather than see visions, you may see pictures unfolding in the surface of the crystal ball, mirror, or water. When this happens, you must interpret what you see. For instance, you might briefly see the head of a female statue and

must decide what it means. Does it literally refer to a statue? Or does it refer to a woman who is the subject of a statue, such as a Greek goddess? If so, does one immediately come to mind, such as Aphrodite? Perhaps if you look up the myth of Aphrodite you'll understand the significance of seeing her head.

Another option, which is commonly experienced by people who read crystal balls, is to see nothing but clouds. If this happens to you, you may decide that white clouds are beneficial and black ones carry warnings, or you might see them in a range of colors, each of which has a different meaning for you.

A crystal ball is thought to be the classic tool for scrying. However, it may not suit you as much as one of the other scrying methods.

SCRYING WITH A BOWL OF WATER

When you first begin to practice scrying, it makes sense to experiment with an inexpensive object such as a bowl or glass of water. If you are successful, you might want to move on to using a crystal ball. However, such objects are expensive and it would be a shame to spend a lot of money on one before knowing whether you are a good scryer.

GETTING STARTED

One good way to start is to fill a tumbler or glass bowl with fresh, clear water and place it on a table in front of you. The glass must be plain, without any decoration such as engravings or writing, as these will be distracting. If you wish, you can bless the water to increase its energetic frequency and you can keep the glass purely for scrying work, so that other people's energies don't come into contact with it.

Choose a time for scrying when you won't be interrupted, then sit in a dimly lit room with the glass or bowl of water in front of you. It may help to prepare yourself with a few minutes of meditation first, so you feel relaxed and receptive. Make sure that you sit out of direct sunlight or harsh artificial lighting because this will distract you from what you are doing.

CLEAR YOUR MIND

Allow your gaze to rest on the surface of the water. Clear your mind of any extraneous thoughts and concentrate entirely on the water. As you do this you'll find that your eyes start to relax and slip slightly out of focus, which will help the scrying process.

If you start to see clouds forming in the glass, this is a very good sign because it shows that something is happening. Alternatively, the water in the glass might remain clear but you could start to see pictures in your mind's eye, in which case you should pay attention to them. There are no right and wrong ways to receive messages from scrying, so you must simply note the way that you respond to it.

Scrying with a bowl of water can take practice before you start to see anything.

SCRYING WITH A MIRROR

The Elizabethan astrologer and magician, John Dee, who was frequently consulted by Elizabeth I, practiced scrying with a mirror. However, it was a special mirror because it had a black back. You can easily create your own version of his mirror by carefully dismantling an ordinary mirror and covering the back of the glass with black paint.

Make sure that you've painted the back of the mirrored glass and not the front! When the paint has dried, you carefully reassemble the mirror.

GETTING STARTED

Ideally you should only use a new mirror when scrying. You should certainly avoid using an old mirror, no matter how decorative it is, if you have bought it second-hand for the specific purpose of scrying. Mirrors are tremendous repositories of energy and you will unwittingly tap into the energy stored in your second-hand mirror, which will affect your readings.

USING A MIRROR

Scrying with a mirror is a very similar process to that of scrying with a bowl of water. You'll get the best results if you sit in a dimly lit room, out of direct sunlight or artificial light. However, you must make sure that you sit at an angle to the mirror so you don't see your own reflection in it. If you can see yourself, you'll become distracted and self-conscious.

As when scrying with water, gaze into the mirror and let your eyes relax. Keep your mind as focused as possible on what you're doing and don't let it drift into mundane thoughts such as what is going to be on television that night. Nevertheless, other ideas may come to you, apparently out of nowhere, and you should pay attention to these because they may have a message for you. For instance, you might suddenly think of a foreign country or a person's name might come to you, and this could turn out to be very significant.

*Sit comfortably and
at an angle to the
mirror, so you can
see its surface
clearly but can't see
your own reflection.*

SCRYING WITH A CRYSTAL BALL

For many people, this is the most obvious way to practice scrying. You can buy crystal balls from specialist shops as well as from the internet. You might also be able to buy them as antiques, but you should be careful about this because traditionally no one should use another person's crystal ball to avoid picking up the other person's energy.

TYPES OF CRYSTAL BALL

You can buy crystal balls in a variety of shapes and sizes. You can choose a crystal ball made from completely clear, flawless crystal. Alternatively, you might prefer one that deliberately contains a flaw, perhaps because it's something for you to focus on and it seems to trigger your intuition. Perhaps you're drawn to a cloudy crystal instead. Another option is to buy a much smaller ball, known as a shew-stone, which is made from a colored crystal such as beryl. It doesn't really matter which sort of crystal ball you choose, provided that you feel comfortable with it and you enjoy working with it. As with any other divination tool, you will soon stop using it if you don't feel a bond with it.

PREPARING THE CRYSTAL BALL

When you've found the right crystal ball for you, you must prepare it for scrying. To do this, wash it in warm, soapy water to remove the energies of anyone else who has touched

Crystal balls are expensive, so you might want to put your scrying skills to the test with a mirror or bowl of water first.

When you first acquire your crystal ball you should clean it of other people's energy.

it. Rinse it well in clear, warm water and then dry it with a soft, lint-free cloth. You must then start to impregnate the crystal with your energy, by handling it frequently and practicing scrying with it. You might also like to dedicate it to scrying, perhaps by holding it and saying, "Crystal ball, I dedicate you to helping me to see into the future. Thank you for working with me."

SCRYING WITH THE CRYSTAL BALL

Scrying with a crystal ball is a very similar process to the one performed with a mirror or glass of water. Sit comfortably, in a dimly lit room, with the crystal ball resting on a table in front of you. Alternatively, you might prefer to hold the ball in the palms of your hands, depending on how large it is. Gaze into its depths and let your eyes relax while concentrating on what you are doing.

Most scryers who use a crystal ball start to see clouds swirling around the inside of the ball after a few minutes. These clouds may be all you ever see inside the crystal ball, in which case you could study their shapes and decide if these have a message for you. On the other hand, the clouds might give way to visions that you either see within the crystal itself or in your mind's eye.

If you feel that you have it in you to be a scryer, you could invest in your own crystal ball.

CLOUD INTERPRETATION

Here are some suggestions of what different colored clouds can mean when they appear in your crystal ball. If the colors are combined, you can combine their meanings accordingly.

White clouds	Good fortune is on the way.
Golden clouds	Prosperity and abundance are signified. Achievement and fame might also be indicated.
Silver clouds	A very favorable sign, indicating the arrival of blessings and riches.
Red clouds	A warning sign, suggesting that you should take great care and avoid any sort of risk.
Orange clouds	You are entering a vibrant, lively phase.
Brown clouds	It will be difficult to see the way forward. Beware of potential pitfalls.
Green clouds	You are entering a fruitful and invigorating phase. It's a time of beginnings.
Blue clouds	Travel is likely, especially over water or in the air.
Black clouds	There is a difficult period ahead. It will be a time when you learn a great deal about yourself.

PART TWELVE

Folk arts

WHAT ARE FOLK ARTS?

Many traditional fortune telling methods are part of the legacy of old folk arts. Some of the divination techniques described in this section are rooted in history and go back thousands of years, while others aren't quite so ancient.

Every technique described in this section has a long and interesting tradition, and many may even have crossed continents. Reading tea leaves, for instance, is a practice that originated in China hundreds of years ago, when people started to interpret the patterns that were formed by the tea leaves left in the bottom of their cups. The art of reading fortunes from tea leaves became popular in the West after tea-drinking was introduced there around the beginning of the 17th century.

FOLK ART FORTUNE TELLING

The techniques in this section of the book range from being very simple to slightly more complicated. Some of them don't need any special equipment at all, while others use objects that you may already have at home, such as dice and dominoes. Some of the techniques require you to perform a certain amount of interpretation yourself while others involve nothing more complicated than reading the printed interpretations.

SYMBOLS

Reading tea leaves, practicing ceromancy (interpreting the shapes of melted wax) and interpreting dreams all require an ability to divine a meaning in a particular symbol, shape or event. You'll find a short directory of meanings at the end of the sections on reading tea leaves and interpreting dreams.

Although many symbols and shapes are included in these two directories, it would be impossible to provide a fully comprehensive list, so you may have to use your intuition when interpreting symbols that aren't mentioned on these pages. Read the other interpretations to get a feel for them, then allow your instincts to guide you toward making the correct interpretation of your symbols.

*Reading tea leaves was a very popular pastime
in the 18th and 19th centuries.*

READING TEA LEAVES

Tasseomancy, to give tea-leaf reading its proper name, is a classic form of divination that has been practiced for centuries. Its popularity has dwindled slightly in recent years because of the rise of the teabag. This might be a convenient way to make a cup of tea but it's hopeless for tasseomancy purposes.

You can't even cut open a teabag to read the leaves because they are too small and uniform in shape to create suitable patterns. If you want to read tea leaves you've got to buy loose tea.

CHOOSING THE RIGHT TEA LEAVES

There are plenty of types of loose tea to choose from, so the sort of tea you buy is literally a matter of taste. However, fruit and herb teas aren't suitable because they don't contain tea leaves. Neither can you use a tea containing petals, such as jasmine. Ideally, you should choose a loose tea with leaves of slightly different sizes, so you'll get a variety of shapes in the bottom of your cup. Cheap blends of tea may not be suitable because the leaves will be small and will tend to clump together. Keemun, Ceylon, Darjeeling, Assam, English Breakfast, Earl Grey, Lady Grey, Kenya, and Oolong are all good teas for tasseomancy.

CHOOSING A TEA CUP AND TEAPOT

You must choose your cup and saucer carefully. Find a cup with a rounded bowl so the liquid tea can swirl around it easily and the tea leaves can stick to it. The cup must also have a plain interior. Patterned cups may be pretty but they'll distract you because you'll find it difficult to distinguish between the tea leaves and the pattern. Your cup must also have a handle because this is an important element in tea-leaf reading.

As for the teapot, it must allow a good flow of tea leaves into the cup, otherwise you won't have enough to interpret. You might therefore want to avoid teapots with inbuilt strainers. You should leave your own tea strainer in the drawer, too.

Choose a cup with a handle as this is an
important element in tea-leaf reading.

Leave the tea to drain out of the cup for at least 30 seconds before starting your reading.

MAKING AND POURING THE TEA

Tradition says that you must drink your tea before interpreting the tea leaves, so it's wise to make tea that you'll enjoy. Use a good teapot, whether china or metal, and freshly boiled water. Warm the pot with a little hot water, then spoon in the loose tea and pour on freshly boiled water. Leave the tea to draw for a few minutes, then pour it into your cup. Once again, tradition has something to say about this, because you are only supposed to read the leaves of the first cup of tea that's poured. However, you can break this rule and read the leaves of everyone present if you wish, provided that there are enough tea leaves to go around.

ASKING YOUR QUESTION

Drink your tea while thinking of the question you want to ask or the theme on which you require insight. When you've finished, there should be only a tiny amount of liquid in the bottom of your cup. Concentrating on your question, take your cup in your non-dominant hand and rotate

it three times in an counterclockwise direction, then turn it upside down on its saucer and leave it to drain for about 30 seconds. When you are sure that all the liquid has drained into the saucer, you can turn the cup up the right way.

LOOKING INTO YOUR CUP

Before you start your reading, you need to gain an overview of the tea leaves in your cup. You might immediately see clear patterns but sometimes all you can see will be a mishmash of shapes that are hard to

Before you start your reading turn the cup around in your hands.

interpret. If you can't determine any recognizable shapes, it helps to half-close your eyes when looking at the leaves as this will make them more clearly defined. Trust your intuition and be patient. Look at the shapes from every angle to see if this helps matters, as you may have been looking at a shape that was originally upside down. If you still can't see anything, it's not the right day for a reading and you must try again another time.

THE SECTIONS OF THE CUP

When you've seen some recognizable shapes, you must determine their position in the cup. That's because tea cups are divided into three sections in tasseomancy, with each section ruling a different period of time. The rim and upper third of the bowl refers to the immediate present and the next couple of days. The middle section of the bowl signifies the next couple of weeks, and the lower third of the bowl and the base represents between two and four weeks into the future.

THE HANDLE

You must also look for shapes that are near the handle, as this represents the person

who is having the reading. The shapes that appear near the handle may describe events that are happening to the person or an aspect of her character. Tea-leaf patterns that are to the left of the handle refer to the past and to events or situations that are leaving the person's life. Tea-leaf patterns to the right of the handle refer to the present and also to the future.

GIVING A READING

Always start reading the leaves from the left of the handle, and work your way round in a clockwise direction. When you first give tea-leaf readings you'll probably be quite hesitant and nervous, but you'll become much more confident with practice. You will also gain a better understanding of how the timing works and become more skilled at seeing patterns in the tea leaves.

It's not a good idea to give yourself a tasseomancy reading more than once a day, but there's nothing to stop you making it a daily ritual. You might even decide to find a special cup and saucer that you use purely for your tasseomancy readings.

Look at the cup from every angle—shapes you didn't notice at first may jump out at you.

TEA LEAF SHAPES

Here is a selection of some of the shapes you can expect to see in your tea cup, and their general meanings. You can adapt these according to the nature of your question. For instance, if a cat appears in a question about love it might mean that someone needs plenty of independence. Use your intuition when interpreting any shapes that aren't mentioned here.

FACE
New people are coming into your life.

CAT
Luck is on the way. It may also be a good time to become more independent.

FLOCK OF BIRDS
You will soon be traveling, whether for business or pleasure. Alternatively, you might have visitors from abroad.

STAR
This is a very positive symbol. It tells you that things are going well and a dream may come true.

FULL MOON
It's the end of a cycle and a time for farewells. Trust that something new will take the place of what's coming to an end.

CHAIN
Work hard at strengthening the link between you and a special person.

ANGEL
You are being looked after by the angelic realms. Trust that everything will work out well for you.

BEE
A busy time is indicated.

COMET

This is a very auspicious symbol because it indicates increased prestige for you.

BUTTERFLY

This represents someone who's flirtatious and light-hearted. It can also indicate a tendency to flit from one activity or interest to the next.

SUN

This is a very encouraging symbol because it signifies creativity, happiness, and radiance for you.

TREE

Spend more time surrounded by nature because it will do you good. You may need to become more grounded.

CLOUDS

You are beset by temporary problems. The good news is that they will soon vanish.

BOWL

You will be offered a beneficial opportunity.

DOG

You can count on someone's fidelity and loyalty. This symbol may also be encouraging you to take more exercise.

CROSS

There are two meanings for a cross. The first is a kiss, which suggests love is on the way. The second is a warning, showing that the path ahead is barred to you.

LINES OF DASHES

These indicate a very busy and lively time in which you'll be moving from place to place.

SCISSORS

Something must be cut out of your life. Do you know what it is?

QUESTION MARK
You're puzzled by a mystery in your life. Look to nearby symbols in the cup for further clues about what this is and how it can be solved.

NEW MOON
There are new beginnings for you. Take a fresh approach to your life.

WINE GLASS
You will soon have something to celebrate. It's also a good time to do some entertaining.

LIGHTNING
A flash of lightning represents a shock that appears to come out of nowhere. It can also indicate a sudden realization.

TWO RINGS
These symbolize some form of union, such as an engagement or marriage.

OWL
Be wise. You are being warned about disappointments and possible betrayals, so be careful about the people you trust.

HEART
Spend time with the people who mean a lot to you. Loving relationships are very satisfying. There could be a new romance.

HAND
You are about to meet someone new. Look for a nearby initial or symbol that will give you a clue about who this person is.

BRIDGE

You are crossing from one chapter in your life to the next. A bridge may also encourage you to make peace with someone.

CURRENCY SYMBOL

Money will soon be on the way to you.

EXCLAMATION MARK

You can expect a surprise.

MUSHROOM

Something in your life is just coming to the surface. Give it time to develop and manifest.

PLUS SIGN

It's time to add something to your life. Look for nearby symbols that tell you what this is.

SHEEP

Don't follow other people's lead without thinking for yourself first. Are you sure you want to copy what they are doing?

FOUR-LEAF CLOVER

This is a very favorable symbol. You'll soon find something that is very rare and precious.

HOUSE

Your domestic life is highlighted. There could be a house move or maybe you must simply devote more time to your home and family.

LADDER

You're making progress. A ladder is especially favorable if your question concerns your career or goals.

FLORAL LORE

Flowers are part of a secret language, whether we know it or not. Hundreds of years ago in the East, lovers sent messages to each other through their choice of flowers and foliage. This allowed them to send very intimate messages of which no one else was aware.

Flowers have continued to be assigned meanings, and the language of flowers, which is known as florigraphy, was especially popular in Victorian times when bridal bouquets were very carefully chosen for their floral meanings.

The Victorians were very enthusiastic about florigraphy and developed a complicated system whereby a flower might mean one thing when it was used alone but something completely different when used in combination with another flower or plant. Today, it's traditional to send red roses on St. Valentine's Day, and red poppies have come to symbolize the massive loss of life in the First World War, but most of us have little knowledge of the meaning of flowers beyond that.

Knowing the meanings of flowers and plants, however, gives them a completely new dimension. Next time you walk into a florist's in the spring and can't resist buying a big bunch of yellow tulips because they look so glorious, you might like to know that they mean "hopeless love." Does that make them more appealing to you or less?

CONTINUING THE TRADITION

One way to use the language of flowers is to send messages to cherished people through the flowers you give them. The lists on the following pages will give you some ideas. If you're planning the flowers for a special event, such as a wedding, you might want to give it added significance by choosing flowers with pertinent meanings. Another option is to plant a garden full of flowers whose meanings you like. Even if you can't run to an entire garden, you could plant a border or a container with flowers that symbolize luck, love, or something else that you want to attract into your life.

Traditionally, brides' bouquets contain flowers with romantic meanings.

THE MEANING OF FLOWERS

Here are some of the many meanings of flowers. Be careful if you want to send secret messages through flowers to other people because this is a selection of meanings and different sources can vary quite dramatically in their interpretations of florigraphy.

A sprig of apple blossom means, as you might expect, fleeting beauty.

TREES

Ash tree	Splendor
Elm	Pride
Apple tree	Knowledge
Walnut	Cleverness
Yew	Sorrow
Aspen tree	Timidity
Box tree	Steadfastness
Broom	Meekness
Hazel	Luck
Oak	Bravery
Fern	Delicacy
Almond, flowering	Hope
Hawthorn	I live in hope
Olive	Peace

Elder	Persistence
Acacia	Friendship
Cherry blossom	A long-lasting friendship
Myrtle	Be my love
Vine	I'm intoxicated by you
Apple blossom	Fleeting beauty
Bay tree	Reward
Larch	Boldness
Beech tree	Prosperity
Holly	Thinking ahead
Juniper	Protection
Blackthorn	Difficulties

FLOWERS

Tulip, red	I declare my love
Carnation, white	My love is pure
Chrysanthemum, red	I love you
Rose, white	I love you
Canterbury bell, blue	My heart is yours
Water lily	Purity of heart
Heliotrope	I adore you
Ivy	I cling to your love
Lilac, purple	You are my first love
Wallflower	Through thick and thin

Amaryllis	Dramatic beauty
Glory flower	Wonderful beauty
Bluebell	I am faithful
Violet, purple	Fidelity
Honeysuckle	Devotion
Ranunculus	Attraction
Marigold, garden	You light up my life
Buttercup	You light up my life
Pink	You're so lovely
Pelargonium, pink	Pretty
Dianthus	Sweetness
Convolvulus	I'll never let you go
Daffodil	I care for you
Geranium, rose-scented	You are special
Carnation, red	I must see you soon
Chrysanthemum, bronze	I am your friend
Tulip, yellow	Hopeless love
Chrysanthemum, yellow	I love another
Foxglove	Do you really care?
Candytuft	I don't care for you
Aster	Second thoughts
Anemone, cultivated	Forgotten
Everlasting flower	I will never forget you
Zinnia	I miss you
Marigold, French	Jealousy

Iris	Pride
Daisy, common	Innocence
Daphne odora	Perfection
Honesty	Honesty
Gardenia	Purity
Snowdrop	Hope
Azalea	Moderation
Dahlia	Instability
Geranium, hardy	Perseverance
Forget-me-not	Steadfastness
Hydrangea	Fickleness
Violet, sweet	Modesty
Lilac, white	Innocence
Primrose	Innocence
Lily, white	Purity
Sweet William	Gallantry
Peony	Shyness
Love-in-a-mist	Confusion
Syringa	Memory
Pansy	Thoughts
Tulip	Celebration
Jasmine	Receptivity
Anemone, wild	Illness
Sweet pea	Subtle pleasures
Acanthus	Clever wiles

The iris is a flower that's associated with pride.

Chrysanthemum, white	I believe in you
Hyacinth	I admire you
Clematis	You're so clever
Sunflower	I will follow you anywhere
Canterbury bell, white	I will treasure your gift
Begonia	Someone is watching us
Pelargonium, red	I'm unsure of you
Cyclamen	I am shy
Marigold, African	You're too brash
Narcissus	You're too egotistical
Carnation, striped	Not yet
Daisy, Michaelmas	Adieu
Guelder rose	Timeless
Hellebore	Gossip
Alyssum, sweet	Prized beyond rubies
Poppy, red	Consolation

HERBS

Nasturtium	Natural beauty
Pomegranate	My soul is yours
Veronica	You are my true love
Auricula	Perfection
Bramble	I don't deserve you
Chickweed	I jump into your arms

A red poppy is used to commemorate the lives of those who have died in battle.

Goldenrod	Give me time to think
Mint	I'm not for you
Witch hazel	Enchantment
Lily of the valley	Joy
Dandelion	Glory
Laurel	Glory
Agrimony	Gratitude
Centaury	Delicacy
Sage	Wisdom
Cowslip	Thoughts
Angelica	Inspiration
Borage	Clumsiness
Thyme	Busyness
Rue	Regret
Aloe	Bitter regret
Aconite	Dislike
Larkspur	Lightness
Rosemary	Remembrance
Camomile	You are full of courage
Kingcup	Craving riches
Basil	I wish you well
Bay leaf	I will never change
Coriander	Hidden worth

SUPERSTITIONS AND TRADITIONS

There are many traditional ways to tell your fortune but some of them are in danger of becoming forgotten. Here are some of the many superstitions and traditions that provide quick glimpses of what the future might hold for you.

Some of the traditions involve asking questions about marriage, which at one time was the only socially acceptable way for two people to live together. That's different today, of course, so you can use these traditions to ask if you'll have a committed relationship with someone, rather than if you'll marry him or her.

APPLE PEELINGS

If you want to discover one of the initials of the man or woman you'll marry, tradition says you can do this with apple peel. You should peel the apple skin into one long strip while thinking about your question. Then toss the apple skin over your left shoulder with your right hand. Without touching it, examine the peel to see if it's fallen in the shape of an initial letter. If so, this is one of the initial letters of your future spouse.

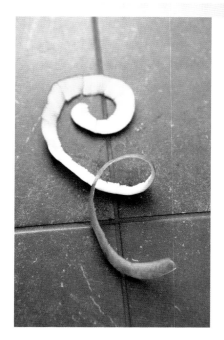

Peel the skin of an apple into one long strip.

WEDDING CAKE

If you are single, the next time you are given a piece of wedding cake you should pass a small fragment of it through a ring three times. Sleep with this tiny fragment of cake under your pillow (wrap it in a tissue to avoid it staining your bedclothes) and you will dream of your future partner.

Throwing the peel over your shoulder will reveal the initials of the person you are going to marry.

HALLOWEEN RITUAL

This ritual is not for the faint-hearted. On the night of Halloween (October 31), you should go into a dark room with only a lighted candle for illumination. Don't switch on the lights. Sit in front of a mirror while combing your hair. After a few minutes you'll see the face of your future partner looking at you over your shoulder.

CHERRY PITS

Next time you eat some cherries, plums, or olives that still have their pits, you can perform this ritual to discover who your next partner will be. When you've finished eating, count the pits while saying one of the following rhymes. If you want to know when you'll marry, count the pits while saying: "This year, next year, sometime, never." If you want to know the profession of the person you'll marry, say: "Tinker, tailor, soldier, sailor, rich man, poor man, beggar man, thief." Alternatively, you could say: "Army, navy, peerage, trade, doctor, divinity, law."

THE RING

This is a technique in which you dowse to discover whether you'll marry. It's important to keep your mind clear while performing the ceremony to avoid influencing the result through wishful thinking. Choose a photograph of the person you love and tie a length of cotton around a ring. With the photograph in front of you, hold the cotton between your thumb and index finger so the ring dangles in front of the photograph. If the ring starts to rotate in a circle, you will marry this person. If it swings back and forth, marriage isn't likely. If the ring doesn't move at all, there will be delays before any marriage is possible.

You can dowse the photograph of your beloved with a ring to find out whether your relationship will lead to marriage.

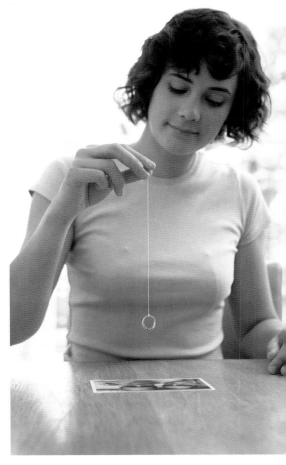

IN THE CARDS

If you are with a group of single friends, you can deal out the cards to find out which of you will marry first. However, this ritual won't work with a mixed-sex group so you must divide the sexes into separate groups. Take a full pack of ordinary playing cards and shuffle them well, then deal out one card to each person in the group, face

Try dealing out the cards to a group of friends to see who will marry first.

down, until all the cards have gone. In a group of women, the woman who's been dealt the King of Hearts will be the first to marry. In a group of men, the man who's been dealt the Queen of Hearts is the one who will marry first.

DICE

Dice were first used in the ancient world, when they were made from the knucklebones of animals and were a tool for divining the future. These earliest dice had four sides, but by the time of the ancient Greek civilization, dice had six sides and some were even made from semi-precious stones. The ancient Greeks used dice for gambling as well as for divination.

Cleromancy, which is the correct term for divination by dice, has been popular for centuries although it has become less well known in recent years. Traditionally, you practice cleromancy with three dice, although you can use two if you prefer. It's usually easy to lay your hands on three dice, even if that means raiding one of the boxed games you usually only drag out of the attic at Christmas.

THE TRADITIONAL RULES

Traditionally, there are a few caveats concerning divining the future with dice. It's up to you whether you follow them or completely ignore them. Alternatively, you might decide to develop your own set of rules. It depends entirely on how you feel about imposing rules on yourself.

Tradition states that you should avoid throwing the dice on Mondays and Wednesdays. When you do throw the dice, you should do so in silence and you should ask someone else to throw the dice for you when you're asking a personal question. You must limit yourself to consulting the dice to once a week. When the dice make a prophecy, it will come true within nine days.

CREATING A CIRCLE

The classic way to cast the dice is to throw them into a circle, about 12 in. (30 cm) in diameter, that you've drawn in chalk on a table or floor. Alternatively, you could draw

Limit yourself to consulting the dice once a week and remember to throw in silence.

the circle on a large sheet of paper or fabric, but make sure that it's flat and unwrinkled, as any unevenness could affect the way the dice fall. If the dice fall inside the circle, you add up their numerical values and consult the interpretation for that number. Tradition decrees that any dice that fall outside the circle must be ignored, but that they indicate quarrels and possibly even separations. If the dice land on top of each other, they're telling you to refuse an opportunity that you've been offered.

The traditional rules of dice are surprisingly strict, which is why you might wish to ignore them. However, if the dice persist in landing outside the circle whenever you throw them, you can safely conclude that it isn't a good time to consult them. Perhaps the situation about which you want advice has already been resolved or has changed in some way that you don't yet know about.

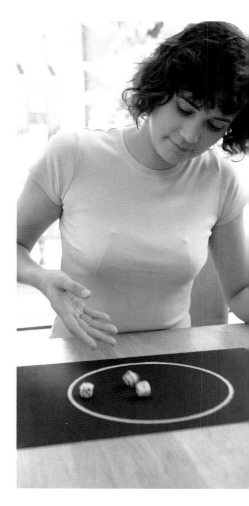

Throwing the dice into a circle gives an extra dimension to your reading.

*Remember that you must ignore any dice that fall
outside the circumference of the circle.*

THROWING THE DICE

When you throw the dice, you can either cup them in your hands or place
them in a special container. If you enjoy using dice, you might like to buy a
special set that you only use for divination purposes. If you are throwing the
dice within a chalk circle, count up the value of all the dice that have fallen
within the circle, then look up the interpretation in this list.

One	This number gives an affirmative answer to any question that you've asked. It only happens when two dice have fallen outside the circle.
Two	This gives a negative answer to any question that you've asked. It happens when one or two dice have fallen outside the circle.

Three	There are some nice but modest surprises coming your way, and there could also be some good fortune around the corner.
Four	The current situation will be beset by difficulties. There could be some disappointing news on its way as well.
Five	A new and unexpected relationship will soon brighten your life. It will be beneficial, enjoyable, and memorable for you.
Six	Don't take situations, people, or possessions for granted because you might risk losing them. Value them and take care of them.
Seven	Take care if your question relates to business matters, because one of the people involved could be treacherous. Only confide in people you trust in order to avoid your secrets becoming the latest gossip.
Eight	The situation is fraught with difficulties because you could soon be made the scapegoat for everything that goes wrong, even if it isn't your fault.
Nine	This is the number of successful and happy relationships, whether they're professional or personal. It's a good time to patch up a quarrel.
Ten	If your question relates to a business, it will be successful. Ten also indicates the birth of something new, such as a relationship or venture.

Eleven	Some form of separation is on the horizon, whether it's permanent or temporary. It will be a poignant experience.
Twelve	Good news is on the way and will be the cause for celebration. If you're considering a job offer you'd be wise to get a second opinion about it.
Thirteen	Thirteen is warning you not to go ahead with the activity connected with your question. Something better will soon come along in its place.
Fourteen	A new friendship is on the way and it will become stronger over time. It promises enjoyment and happiness, and possibly even an emotional commitment.
Fifteen	Play by the rules and don't take risks that could get you in trouble. Listen to your conscience and abide by your principles, even if that's an unexciting option.
Sixteen	An unexpected journey or vacation will be good fun. It may also have benefits that you aren't aware of at first.
Seventeen	You need to be flexible and adapt your plans so they'll fit in with those of others. A business enterprise could be profitable.
Eighteen	This number only comes up when you throw three sixes within the circle. Therefore, it promises many blessings and much joy, as well as promising that a wish will be granted. It gives an affirmative answer to your question.

DOMINOES

Most homes have a set of dominoes tucked away in a cupboard somewhere, even if they're only brought out at Christmas, so this form of divination doesn't need any special equipment.

However, if you enjoy reading your future with dominoes and you become especially skilled at it, you might like to buy yourself a special set of dominoes that you only use for divination purposes. Equally, you might like to buy or make a special cloth on which to place the dominoes whenever you give a reading.

THE HISTORY OF DOMINOES

Dominoes are thought to have originated in China in the 12th century CE. Closely related to dice, early sets of dominoes displayed all the numerical combinations that are created by throwing two dice, with each half of each domino representing one dice. The popularity of dominoes gradually spread from China and reached Italy in the early 18th century. France and Britain were introduced to the game shortly afterward. By this time, there was a marked difference between Chinese and European dominoes, as the latter sets included seven extra dominoes. These consisted of each of the six numbers combined with a blank, plus a double blank. Their official name is a double-six set.

If you enjoy working with dominoes, you may decide to buy yourself a special set.

Use your special set of dominoes purely for fortune-telling purposes.

If the idea of fortune-telling with dominoes appeals to you, you might like to buy a special set or even an antique set. If you find an old set that you like, make sure that it contains all 28 dominoes before you buy it. Otherwise it's useless for divination.

DIVINATION WITH DOMINOES

Reading your future from a set of dominoes comes under the category of cleromancy, which is the art of divination from small objects. The best way to read the dominoes is to lay them out on a flat surface, face down. You can then move them around slightly while thinking of the question you want to ask them. When you are ready, you can either select a single domino to provide

Selecting two or three dominoes will give you readings on different areas of your life.

the answer to your question or you can choose two or three dominoes to represent the different areas of your life for which you need guidance. For instance, you could choose three dominoes to give you information about each of your three children or about three of your friends.

INTERPRETING THE DOMINOES

Here are the traditional meanings of the 28 dominoes in a double-six set.

Blank-blank

Of all the dominoes in the set, this is the one you want to see least. There is a karmic quality to this domino because it describes the difficult results of past actions, often leading to delays and disappointments. Monitor your behavior to prevent yourself creating more unhelpful repercussions in the future.

One-blank

Situations are not quite what they seem and you should be wary of taking people's promises at face value because they may not be able to fulfill them. Be particularly careful where financial arrangements are concerned.

One-one

This is a very fortunate domino because it describes harmony and balance in all areas of life. Difficulties will melt away, apparently solving themselves. It's a good time to make swift but informed decisions and to trust that you are doing the right thing in the process.

Two-blank

Gain a proper perspective of any problems that you are facing by looking at them as objectively as possible. Assess them from every angle so you gain a full understanding of what has caused the problems and how to solve them. Travel is favorable and could lead to a new relationship.

Two-one

A relationship could help to improve your financial position in some way. Alternatively, you will simply enjoy a harmonious rapport with the people around you. Sometimes this domino describes a reunion with an old friend.

Two-two

The best way to make progress in business and money matters is to take things slowly and carefully. If you do this you will enjoy great success and satisfaction, not only on a professional level but also in your personal life.

Three-blank

Watch out for disputes and disagreements. These will seem to arise for no good reason, although it's quite likely that they've been brewing for some time and you've simply been unaware of them. You may also have to cope with a partner who's being reckless or irresponsible.

Three-one

If you have asked the dominoes a question, this tile is traditionally said to give a negative response. It is also telling you that people are being unreliable or untrustworthy, and that you should be circumspect when dealing with them.

Three-two

This isn't a good time to take any kind of risk. However, if you are careful and play safe, everything will go well for you. Relationships, travel, and financial investments are particularly favorable right now.

Three-three

Financially, it's a very beneficial time for you. You can expect to receive large sums of money, possibly from several different sources. Unfortunately, this financial success could cause problems in your relationships, with the potential for jealousy.

Four-blank

It isn't a good time to discuss anything secret because you might accidentally divulge more than you intended, leading to disputes with people who feel you've betrayed their confidence and gone behind their back.

Four-one

Traditionally, this domino advises you to pay off any debts while you've got the means to do so, because money may soon be scarce. Generally speaking, you should save your money rather than spend it.

Four-two

Be careful in all financial matters and show great discrimination when placing your trust in people. This isn't a good time to take risks. Unexpected changes will help to improve your life.

Four-three

Adopt a positive attitude in the face of your current problems. Being optimistic and anticipating a good outcome will help to attract favorable circumstances, and you'll find that things aren't nearly as difficult as you'd feared.

Four-four

Be spontaneous whenever possible and don't try to control situations. This is a very positive domino because it promises happiness and contentment, and is telling you to concentrate on enjoying yourself whenever possible.

Five-blank

A friend needs your help and sympathy, as well as your advice and suggestions, but you've got to choose your words carefully to avoid saying the wrong thing. Show caution and restraint in financial matters.

Five-one

It's a busy time for you socially, with plenty of enjoyable activities to keep you fully occupied. One social event could lead to a new relationship which will start very quickly. Although it will be very promising at first it could soon start to go downhill.

Five-two

This domino has several meanings. Traditionally, it signifies the birth of a child. It can also suggest that you cultivate a more patient attitude. Finally, it can sometimes describe a very happy and busy social life.

Five-three

All is well and you have every reason to feel contented and happy with your lot. It may also be a prosperous time for you financially. Friends and partners are helpful, gregarious, and supportive, and may also offer some good advice.

Five-four

This isn't a good time to overspend or to be reckless with your money, even though you may be feeling prosperous at the time of the reading. Money could arrive from official channels, such as a government agency.

Five-five

It's important to go with the flow and to allow changes to take place in your life. Clinging on to your current circumstances or being resistant to change will lead to many problems and frustrations. Trust that everything will work out for the best.

Six-blank

Take care to avoid gossiping, even if you have a delicious secret that you'd love to broadcast to everyone around you. You should also ignore any gossip that you hear because it may be misleading or malicious.

Six-one

This tile traditionally signifies a wedding, although it can also point to some other form of emotional commitment such as a couple moving in together. It can also refer to a spiritual pledge. Sometimes, this domino indicates that problems will melt away.

Six-two

It's essential that you behave in an ethical manner and don't do anything that you'll come to regret. Your good behavior will be rewarded by some fantastic opportunities or a welcome gift. However, you'll have to face the consequences if you aren't honest with someone.

Six-three

This is an excellent time for travel because it will bring you many benefits, including enjoyment and the possibility of a new relationship or important business contact. If you are going on vacation you'll have an especially good time.

Six-four

Be prepared for a brief dispute or disagreement with a friend, colleague or partner. Happily, it will soon be resolved and it may even lead to a greater understanding of one another. Sometimes this domino warns of a tricky legal matter.

Six-five

This domino can indicate a change in status. For instance, it can describe someone who is promoted at work or who becomes a parent. Close friends will bring you many blessings. They are good company, supportive and they might also return a favor.

Six-six

This is the most favorable domino of all. It refers to all forms of abundance, including emotional, financial, professional, and spiritual prosperity. There is often a good reason to celebrate when this domino appears.

CEROMANCY

For thousands of years, people have tried to glimpse the future through ceromancy. In this technique, you ask a question and then melted wax is tipped into a bowl of water and allowed to set. When it's solid, you carefully remove the wax from the water and interpret the meaning of its shape. This interpretation provides the answer to your question.

When you practice ceromancy you can feel how ancient it is because it has such a timeless quality. It is easy to imagine the ancient Greeks and Egyptians doing exactly the same thing in their quest to discover what the future held for them. In fact, it is one of the oldest forms of divination in this entire book.

PREPARING FOR THE RITUAL

Ceromancy may be a very simple technique but it does need a certain amount of preparation and forethought. First, you must choose your candle carefully. Look for a large, wide candle in a strong color; white isn't suitable because it can be difficult to see the exact shape of the wax when it has set. The candle must be sturdy enough to burn for at least an hour before you're ready to perform the ceromancy ritual, to

give it enough time to accumulate a generous amount of melted wax. You need one candle for each question, so if you want to ask three questions it's advisable to light all three candles at the same time to avoid long delays.

You must also choose a suitable bowl in which to tip the wax. It can be made from glass, china, or metal, but it must be in a contrasting color to that of the candle so you can see exactly what you're doing.

ASKING THE QUESTION

When the candle has burned for at least an hour and there is a good pool of melted wax in the top of it, you are ready to perform the ceromancy ritual. At this stage,

Ceromancy is one of the oldest forms of divination known to man.

We humans have always felt a need to know what the future holds for us.

very cold or iced, to encourage the wax to set quickly.

When you feel ready to ask your question, you can either do so out loud or silently. Concentrate very strongly on the question and then carefully extinguish the flame of the candle to prevent it burning your fingers. As soon as you've done this, and while thinking of your question, pick up the candle and tip the wax into the center of the bowl so it drops into the water. Take care not to get the hot wax on your fingers.

Keep thinking of your question while you wait for the wax to set. Don't let your thoughts stray. The wax shape will be ready to interpret after a few minutes.

you might like to set the scene by dimming the lights or lighting some other candles, by sitting quietly for a few minutes to mentally prepare yourself for the ceremony and perhaps by playing some quiet and evocative music. Such activities help to put you in the right frame of mind for what will follow. Besides, having waited for at least an hour for the candle to be ready it seems a shame to rush through the next part of the ritual. Fill the bowl with water that is either

INTERPRETING THE WAX SHAPE

When you're ready, study the wax shape from every angle while it's still in the water. You may have to be slightly creative about this and it can help if you look at the shape through half-closed eyes because this gives it more definition. Sometimes its shape will immediately suggest something to you. For instance, it might form an initial letter that has particular relevance to the question you asked. However, sometimes it's hard to interpret the wax shape, at which point it will be helpful to lift it out of the water so you can study it more closely. Refer to the directories of symbols at the end of the tea-leaf reading and dreams sections (pages 340–343 and pages 380–387 respectively) for guidance on what your shape might mean. When you lift the wax out of the water, make sure that it's completely set otherwise it will break or change shape.

If you want to ask more than one question, finish interpreting the shape formed by the first candle before pouring the wax from the next one into the bowl.

You may find it useful to lift the wax shape out of the water in order to study it more closely.

CANDLES

Telling the future from the behavior of candle flames is called lynchnomancy. It's an easy and uncomplicated form of divination, and is very evocative of ancient times when candles were the only form of illumination in a house. However, when you practice lynchnomancy you must make sure that you don't leave the candles burning unattended.

You will be paying attention to the way the candle flames move, so you must place the candles away from any drafts. For instance, you'll get a distorted response if you place the candles near an open window. Ideally, you should practice lynchnomancy in a room in which the windows and doors are closed.

Always use three identical candles when practicing lynchnomancy. The candles should be unused.

THE THREE-CANDLES METHOD

Choose three identical candles, none of which has been lit before. Place them in identical candlesticks or light each one so it creates a little wax, then use this hot wax to anchor the base of the candle to a saucer. Arrange the candles in the shape of a triangle in the center of a table and light them. Then sit quietly and watch the flames to see what happens next, while thinking of your question. Remember to keep the candles away from drafts.

- If one flame burns brighter than the others, you'll have good luck.

- If one flame gutters and flickers, there will be a minor loss.

- If one flame goes out, there will be a serious loss or a major setback.

- If two flames flicker, there will be a surprise in your life.

- If two flames flare up, you'll be offered new opportunities.

- If two flames go out, your life will go through a dramatic phase.

- If all three flames flicker, your circumstances will change for the better.

- If all three flames go out, you'll experience life-changing events.

- If all three flames burn steadily, you'll make good progress in all areas of your life.

- If all three flames flare up, you'll have an unexpected triumph.

DREAMS

Throughout the centuries there have been many stories of dreams that have foretold the future. These stories are drawn from all cultures, countries, and beliefs, which proves that there is a universal and timeless need to delve into the secrets of our dreams and start to unravel them.

You will understand this need yourself if you've ever woken from a dream that seemed significant and wondered what it meant. The following pages may help you.

REMEMBERING YOUR DREAMS

The first step in interpreting your dreams is to remember them. You may have to train yourself to do this because many people don't have total recall of their dreams.

A dream journal

Keep a dream journal in which you always write down your dreams as soon as you've woken up, even if you can only remember fleeting fragments. Doing this will train

Lie still when you wake up, as this will help you to remember your dreams.

your subconscious to hold on to more dream memories and you will soon be able to remember your dreams in great detail. At first, you may want to write down your dreams in the middle of the night, in order to capture them, so keep a pad of paper and a pen by your bed. Jot down as much of the dream as you can remember, otherwise in the morning you may be left wondering what "Five oranges, broken armchair and helicopter" actually means.

Lie still

If you've ever woken with a dream vivid and fresh in your memory, and then got out of bed and instantly forgotten the entire dream, you'll know how important it is to record your dreams before they vanish. One excellent way to encourage this process is to avoid moving after you've woken up. Stay lying in the same position and run through your dream in your head. Make sure that you've got it fixed in your memory, then write it in your dream notebook. Don't let yourself think of anything else in the meantime, such as wondering what the day will bring or what to have for breakfast.

Some dreams can seem more significant than others, so always pay particular attention to dreams that are very vivid, almost seem real or have an epic quality to them. These are the dreams that are most likely to carry an important message.

Keep a special journal for recording your dreams, and your interpretation of them.

TELLING THE FUTURE FROM DREAMS

One of the most common ways to interpret dreams is to do so from a psychological viewpoint. Patients undergoing psychotherapy are often encouraged to discuss their dreams and to analyze them in order to gain greater insight into the workings of their unconscious.

Divining the future from dreams is an entirely different process. It frequently ignores the psychological dimension of dreams and simply concentrates on the traditional meaning of many of the symbols that occur in dreams.

DREAM CALENDAR

Traditionally, you should not only take into account the meaning of your dream but also the day of the month on which you dreamed it.

Date	Interpretation	Date	Interpretation
1	Any bad luck predicted by your dream will reverse itself.	5	Any good fortune predicted by the dream will reverse itself.
2	Your dream won't come true.	6	Your dreams will come true.
3	Very favorable; things are going well for you.	7	Don't reveal the content of your dreams to anyone.
4	The events you dream of will bring you problems.	8	Be patient; happiness will arrive eventually.

Date	Interpretation
9	Your desires will be fulfilled.
10	You'll face difficulties.
11	Your dream will come true in four days' time.
12	Life will be difficult.
13	Your dreams are starting to become reality.
14	A wish will be granted.
15	Be patient.
16	Your dream will come true in 28 days' time.
17	Friends will deceive you.
18	Keep the content of your dreams to yourself.
19	Your dreams will come true in ten days' time.
20	You're promised great happiness.
21	Expect to hear some very good news.

Date	Interpretation
22	There will soon be a dip in your fortunes.
23	Help will come from an unexpected direction.
24	A confusing dream will become much clearer in four days' time.
25	Some money is on the way.
26	Your deepest desires will soon be fulfilled.
27	Don't give up hope.
28	Be choosy about the people you trust.
29	Don't reveal your secrets to a soul.
30	A phone call will be important.
31	You'll hear good news tomorrow.

DREAM INTERPRETATIONS

Over the next few pages, you will find some traditional interpretations of dreams.

PLACES AND OBJECTS

Orchestra	It's lucky to dream of an orchestra playing because you'll be part of a successful team.
Advertisement	If you dream that you are reading an advertisement you'll hear good news. If you dream of placing an advertisement, you'll have problems from which others will have to rescue you.
Treasure	Dreaming that you are searching for treasure means that someone doesn't deserve your love. However, if you dream of finding treasure it means that your relationship is steady and satisfying.
Auction	This is a warning that you are living beyond your means. You could lose something valuable.
Keys	A door is opening up for you.
Bells	Good news is on the way.

Dreaming of a bell shows that you will soon hear some fortunate news.

Cage

To dream that you've released birds from a cage means a marriage proposal or success in business.

Gloves

You are keeping someone at a distance. If you lose a glove, someone close to you will leave your life.

Jewelry

Good fortune is on the way.

Ring

Traditionally, this indicates an engagement or marriage. If you are wearing the ring on your thumb or index finger, you'll have lots of power.

Rings in a dream are a classic symbol of marriage or some other close commitment.

School

To dream that you are teaching at school is a sign of progress and success. To dream that you are being taught at school indicates a setback or the need to acquire more knowledge.

Tower

This is a sign of good fortune, especially if you are climbing the tower. If you are descending it, or you see it fall down, you'll encounter bad luck.

Balcony

Watching people from a balcony indicates success and achievement. If you dream of a balcony collapsing, your plans will fall apart.

Window	If you are looking out of the window you'll receive news from far away. If you are looking at an unpleasant scene, the news will be bad. If the scene is pleasant, the news will be good.
Yacht	Don't be extravagant.
Zoo	Be wary of some of your friends.
Ladder	You will be given a chance to go up in the world if you are climbing the ladder. If you are descending the ladder, you'll face a disappointment.

Take note of whether you're ascending or descending if you dream of a ladder.

PEOPLE AND ACTIONS

Teeth	Dreaming that your teeth are falling out foretells money problems. Dreaming that you are cutting new teeth indicates that you'll learn a new skill. There may also be news of a pregnancy.

Journey	Great changes are in the offing. Time will tell whether these are fortunate or not.
Baby	Dreaming of a baby means good luck and a celebration.
Kiss	This is a very fortunate omen.
Dancing	Social pleasures and enjoyment. If you dream that you are dancing by yourself, you'll achieve success without anyone's help.
Death	It's a lucky omen to dream of a death. It indicates fortunate changes and sometimes foretells a wedding.
Fall	To dream that you're falling indicates insecurity and anxiety.
Hair	It's lucky to dream about a bald man. Dreaming that you've got glossy hair is also lucky. If you dream that your hair is thinning, you should wait for a more auspicious time before beginning a new project.
Laughter	It's very lucky to dream of laughter. It means you'll be successful and happy.
Swimming	It's very lucky to dream that you are swimming strongly through the water. However, problems in swimming indicate worries and disappointments.
Naked	Dreaming that you are naked means that you are too frank with other people.

ANIMALS AND BIRDS

Animals
To dream of friendly animals, such as pets, means a happy domestic life. To dream of wild animals means that trouble will come from your enemies.

Ants
Dreaming of a thriving anthill indicates success in business. It can also indicate a very busy and sociable time, or a happy marriage. If you dream that an anthill was destroyed it means that your plans will be ruined.

Cat
Dreaming of a cat walking by itself foretells a journey. A purring cat indicates hypocrisy; a cat that meows or scratches itself suggests the betrayal of friends.

Dog
If a dog bites you, your best friend will betray you. If the dog barks at you, you'll quarrel with your friend. If the dog is friendly, a friendship will blossom.

Elephant
There will be news from abroad about an old friend.

Frog
You will have a big surprise, possibly connected with love.

Horse
A brown or black horse means news from far away. A piebald horse means a wish will come true. A gray horse means your plans will be delayed. A white horse means a new love.

Nightingale
Dreaming of a nightingale's song indicates that good news is on the way.

Pig
An immensely lucky dream; you'll hear good news and things will go well for you.

| Snake | Be choosy about who you trust. To dream of killing a snake means you'll overcome your problems. |
| Spider | A large spider shows needless worries. A small spider means that money is on the way. |

FOOD

Banquet	There are good times ahead, with plenty of laughter and friendship.
Cooking	There will be an unexpected success.
Eggs	Something hidden will soon be revealed to you. You'll receive many social invitations as well.
Fruit	Prosperity, cheerfulness, and good health.
Honey	Dreaming that you are eating honey is very lucky. You'll have a long and productive life.
Meat	Dreaming of meat indicates that loss and sorrow are on the way. Buying or selling meat, however, is a fortunate sign.

Fruit represents an abundance of happiness.

Milk	To dream that you are drinking milk shows that you are practical and efficient.
Olives	You'll hear reassuring news from a friend.

NATURE

Clouds	Dark clouds mean anger and trouble. White clouds indicate prosperity. Red clouds indicate danger. Clouds that are very high in the sky suggest travel to foreign countries.
Flowers	If you dream of picking flowers, one of your projects will be successful. Wilting or dead flowers indicate failed dreams and plans.
Ice	You are dearly loved by someone.
Moon	Any dreams about the Moon are favorable. Your troubles will soon be over.
Plant	If a plant grows before your eyes it indicates that a project will develop quickly.
Quicksand	Be careful because you may be straying into dangerous or treacherous territory.
Rain	Be prudent with your money.
Rainbow	A very fortunate omen which shows that you'll receive good news and there will be a happy ending to all your enterprises.

Vine

To dream of a flourishing vine means that life is blossoming for you, with money on the way. To dream that you are picking grapes means that your dearest wish will come true. However, you'll have bad luck if you dream of a dead vine.

Volcano

Your circumstances are changing in a dramatic fashion. If you feel imprisoned by your current situation you'll soon break free from it.

Water

Dreaming of muddy or dirty water is a sign that bad luck is on its way to you. Dreaming of clear, fresh water means that you'll be happy. Rough water indicates problems that you must overcome.

MYTHOLOGY

Dragon

Major change is on the way that will transform your life.

Giant

Dreaming about a giant indicates a fear of authority. You may need to scale down your commitments.

To dream of a rainbow promises that you will soon hear good news.

INDEX

Page numbers in *italics* refer to illustrations.

ACKNOWLEDGMENTS

Special Photography: © Octopus Publishing Group Limited/Russell Sadur

Other Photography and Illustrations:
Alamy/Ace Stock Limited 381; /ImageState 384; /Miguel Angel Muñoz Pellicer 14–15; /The Print Collector 276; /Visual Arts Library (London) 271. **akg-images** 286. **Corbis** 123, 174–5, 182, 350, 377; /Artiga Photo 188; /Randy Faris 107; /S. Hammid 296; /Joe McDonald 292–3; /Michael Prince 307; /Roger Ressmeyer 49; /Larry Williams 105; /Zoe/zefa 169. **Digital Vision** 109, 111, 382. **Getty Images** 119, 280; /Altrendo 115; /Davies and Starr 26; /Mark Davis 316; /Karen Moskowitz 121; /Jonathan Nourok 386; /David Oliver 131; /Bob Thomas 124–5; /Roger Tully 290–1; /VEER Florian Franke 283. **Image Source** 282. **Lo Scarabeo** 140–1, 142–3, 144–5, 146–7, 148–9, 150–1, 152–3, 154–5, 156–7, 158–9, 160–1, 162–3, 165. **Octopus Publishing Group Limited** 34, 36; /Kuo Kung Chen 207, 208–9, 211, 212-3, 215, 217, 219, 221, 223, 225; /Vanessa Davies 314; /Tommaso D'Incalci 21, 23, 25, 27, 29, 31, 33, 35, 37, 39, 41, 43, 46–47; /Nicola Gregory 340–1, 342–3; /Jerry Harpur 349; /Rhian Nest Jones 56, 57, 59, 60, 61, 62, 64, 66, 68, 70, 72, 74, 76, 78, 80, 82, 84; /Andy Komorowski 20, 22, 28, 38, 40, 42; /Peter Myers 383; /Mike Prior 306, 308, 309, 312; /Peter Pugh-Cook 204; /Guy Ryecart 24, 30, 32, 232; /Russell Sadur 9, 10, 102, 117, 138, 139, 206, 311, 313, 315, 321, 335, 336, 337, 339, 376; /Mark Winwood 13. **Photodisc** 45, 52, 53, 179, 278–9. **Photolibrary Group** 345. **Science Photo Library**/Mehau Kulyk 51. **The Art Archive**/Museo Capitolino Rome/Dagli Orti 100; /Private Collection/Marc Charmet 137. **Topfoto** 19; /Werner Forman 295; /Charles Walker 228–9, 333.

Executive Editor   Sandra Rigby
Editor   Emma Pattison
Executive Art Editor   Sally Bond
Designer   Julie Francis
Photographer   Russell Sadur
Production Controller   Audrey Walter